People and Places

pastel paintings

by Elena Malec

Artist Statement

The series of paintings "People and Places" originated with my travel photos taken across continents in the countries I visited.

The goal of painting in pastel scenes from diverse cultures is to create frescoes of life with an atmosphere typical to a moment in time.

The message of these scenes of life is one of peace and tolerance, respect for different beliefs, different lifestyles and ethnic diversity.

There is a beauty and vibration of life everywhere on earth.

The composition of each piece is meant to emphasize the truth, validity, moral values and respect for all religions and ways people choose to adopt in their culture or part of the world they live.

My series "People and Places" is a manifesto of the right we all have to live, work, worship.

What better language than that of art for a heartfelt message of peace and harmony among people.

Elena Malee

2

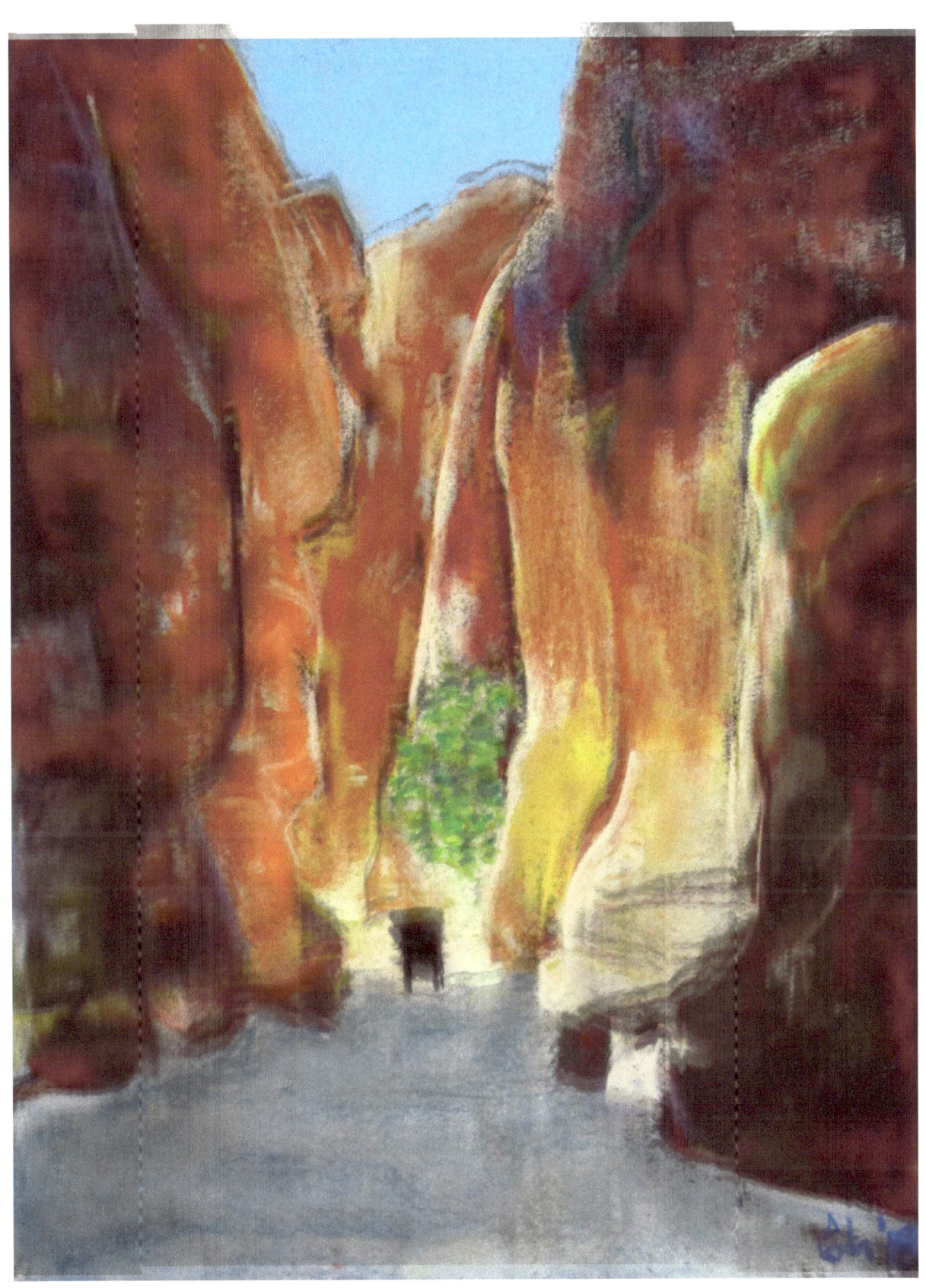

A Calesh in Petra, Jordan
A Calesh in Petra, Jordan

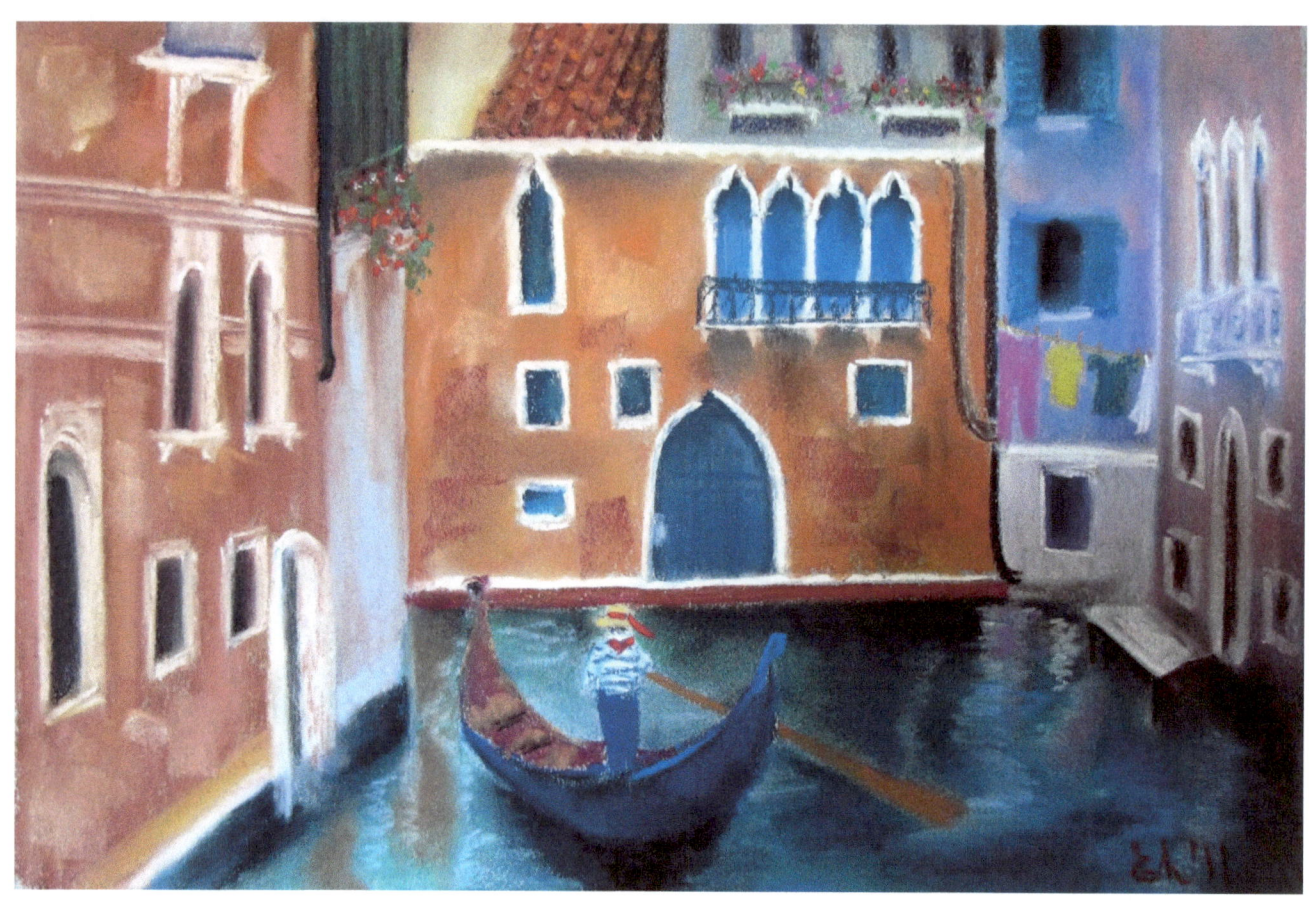

A Gondola in Venice, Italy

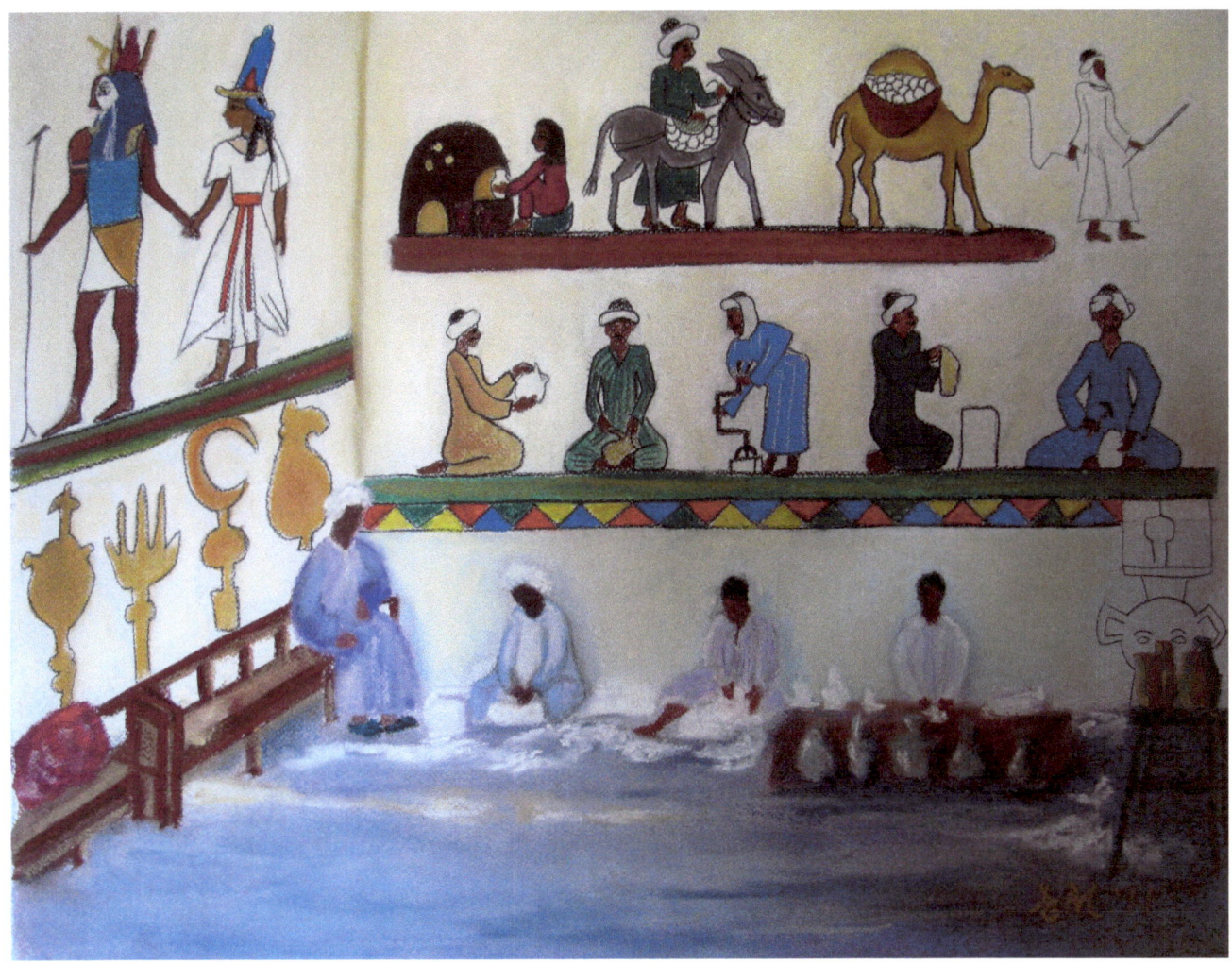

Alabaster workers in Luxor, Egypt

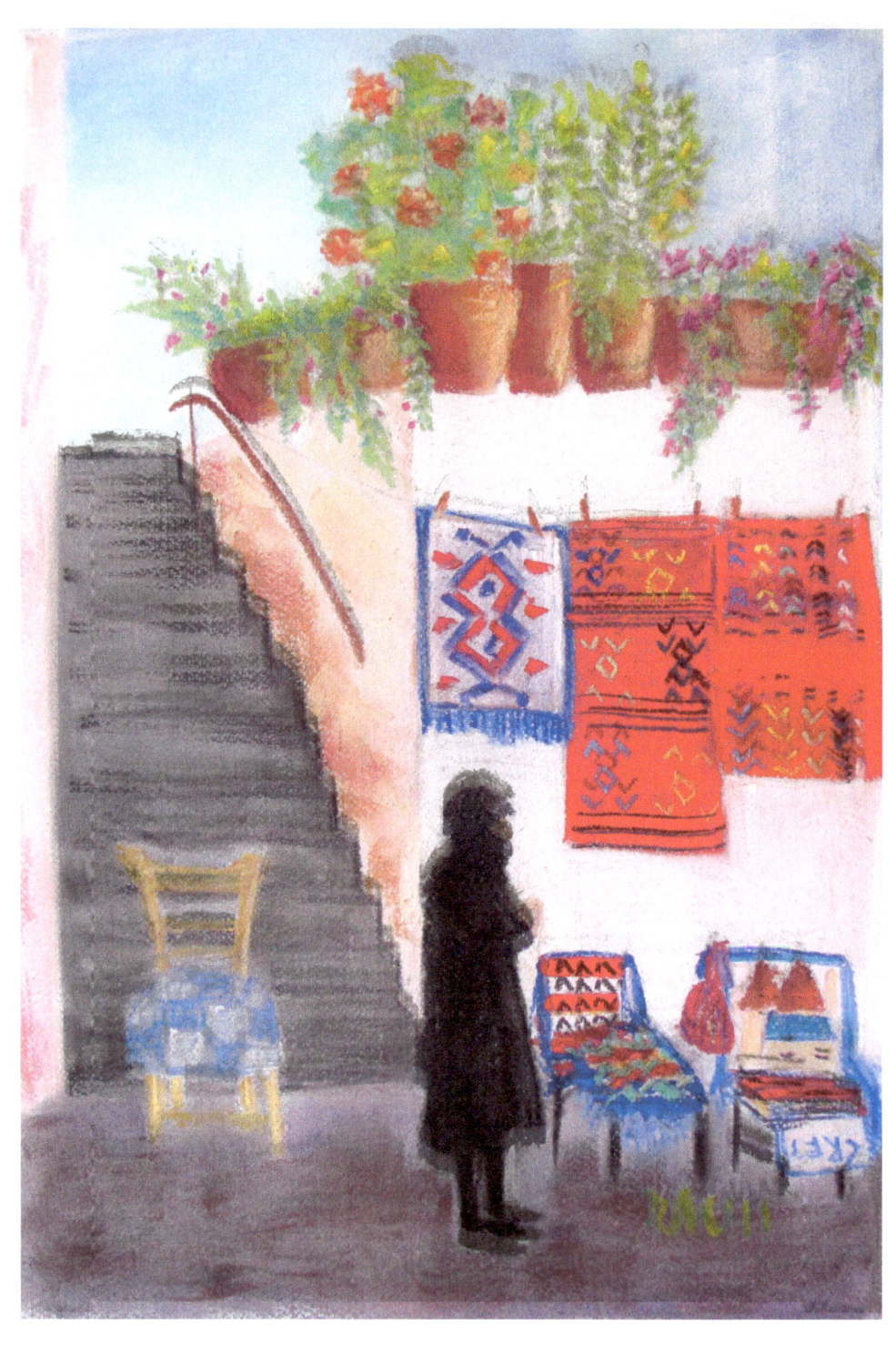

Rugs for sale, Anogia, Crete, Greece.
Rugs for sale; Anogia; Crete; Greece:

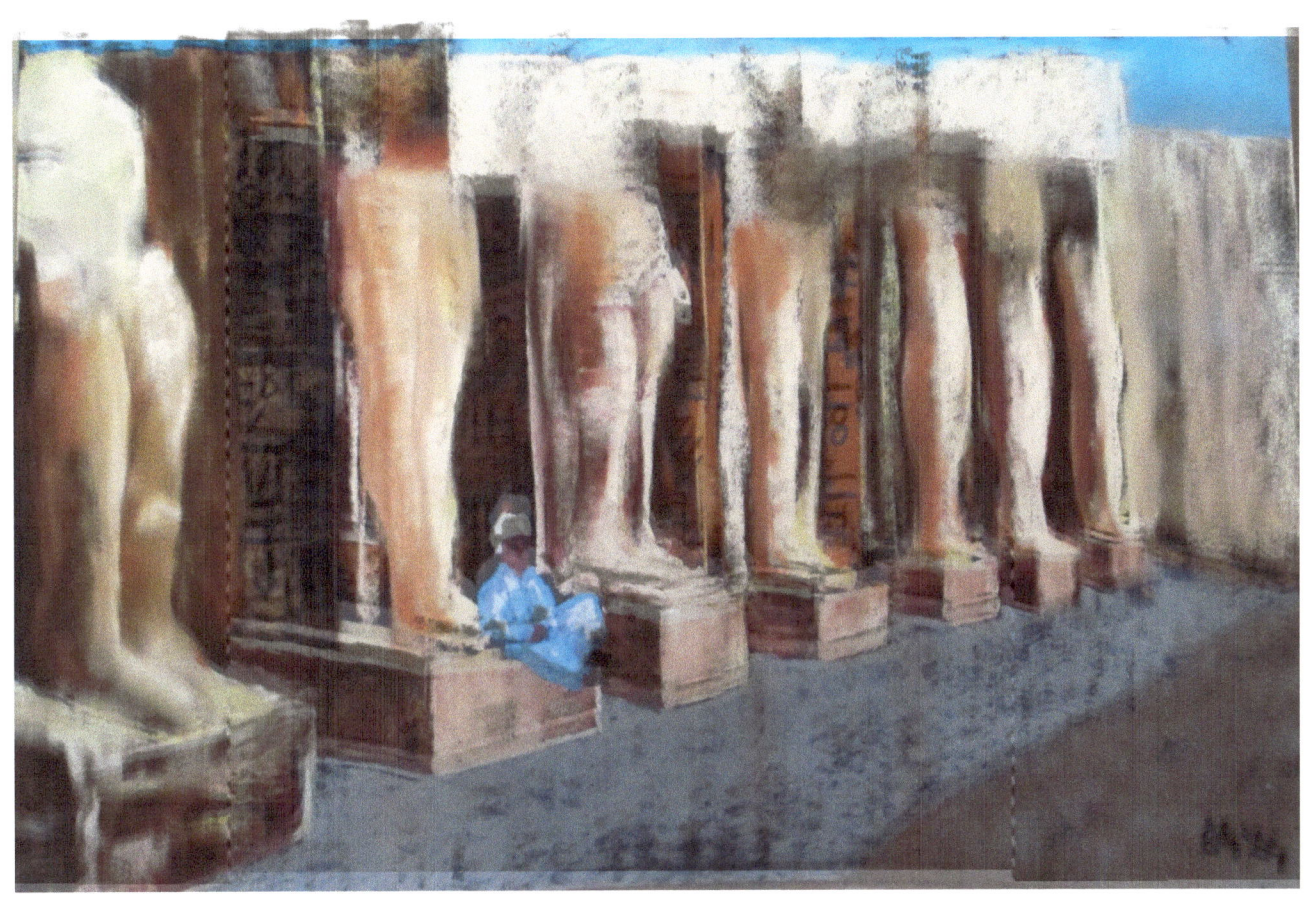

At Karnak, Luxor, Egypt

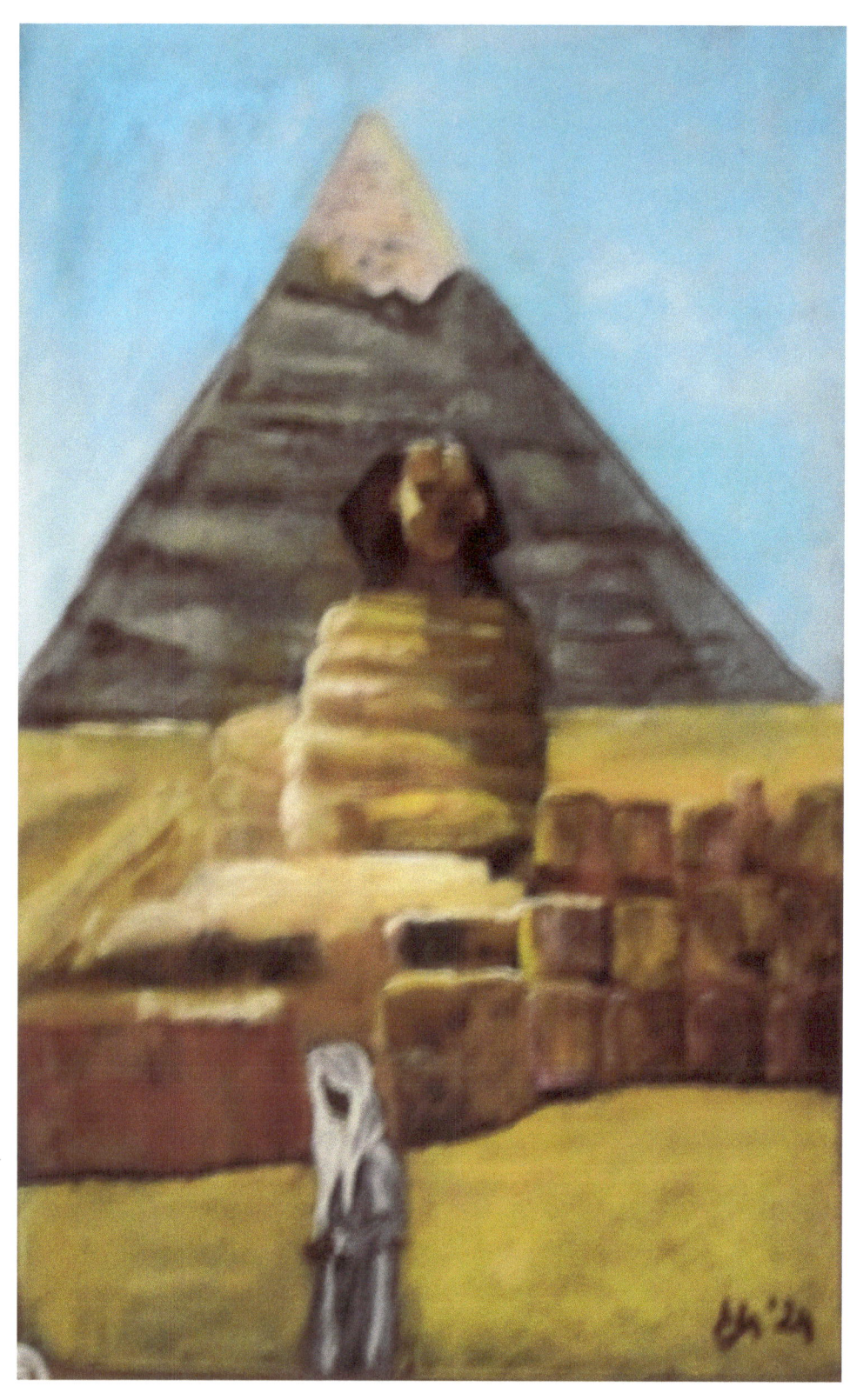

Bedouin at Giza, Egypt

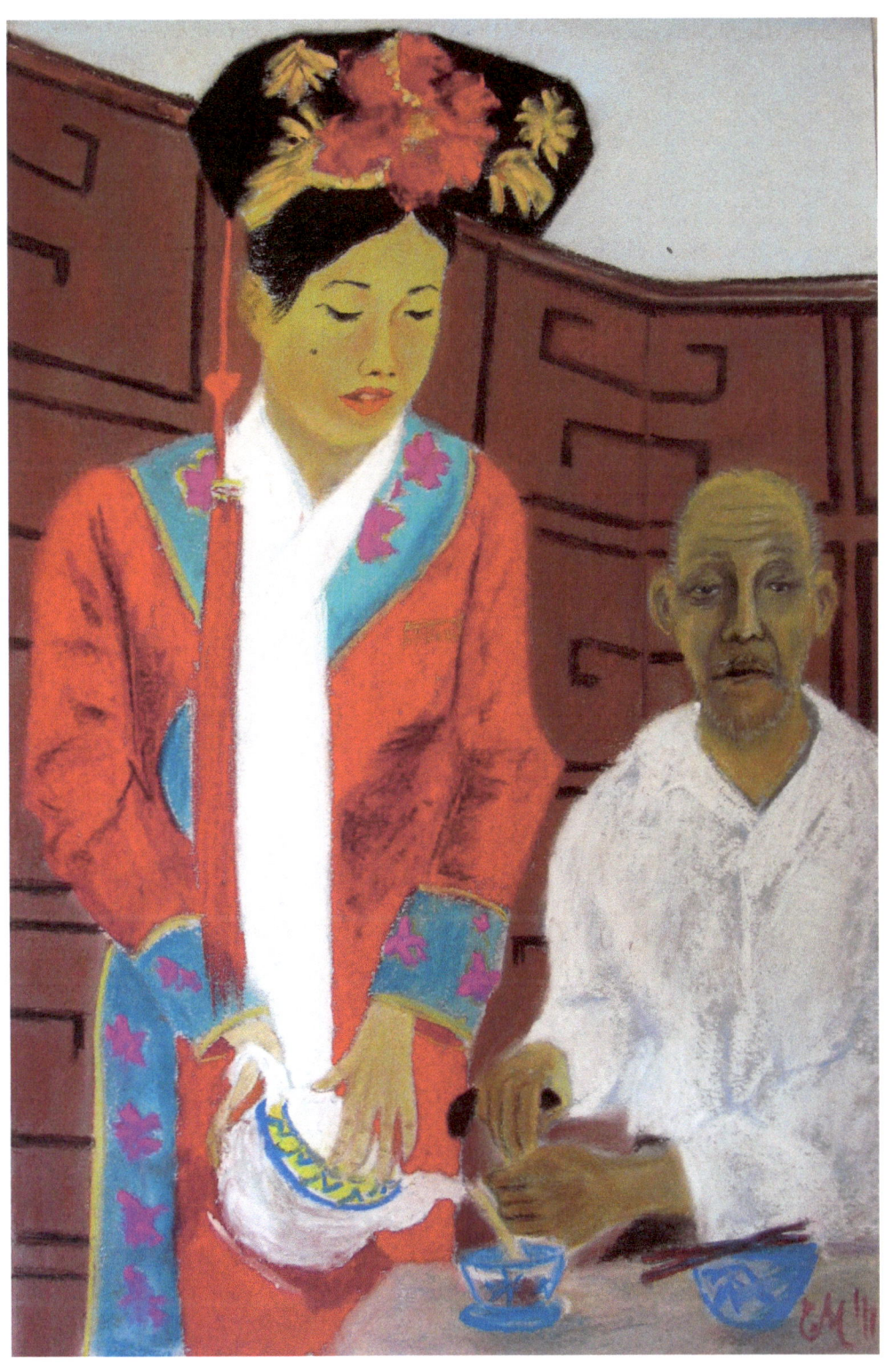

Beijing waitress, China

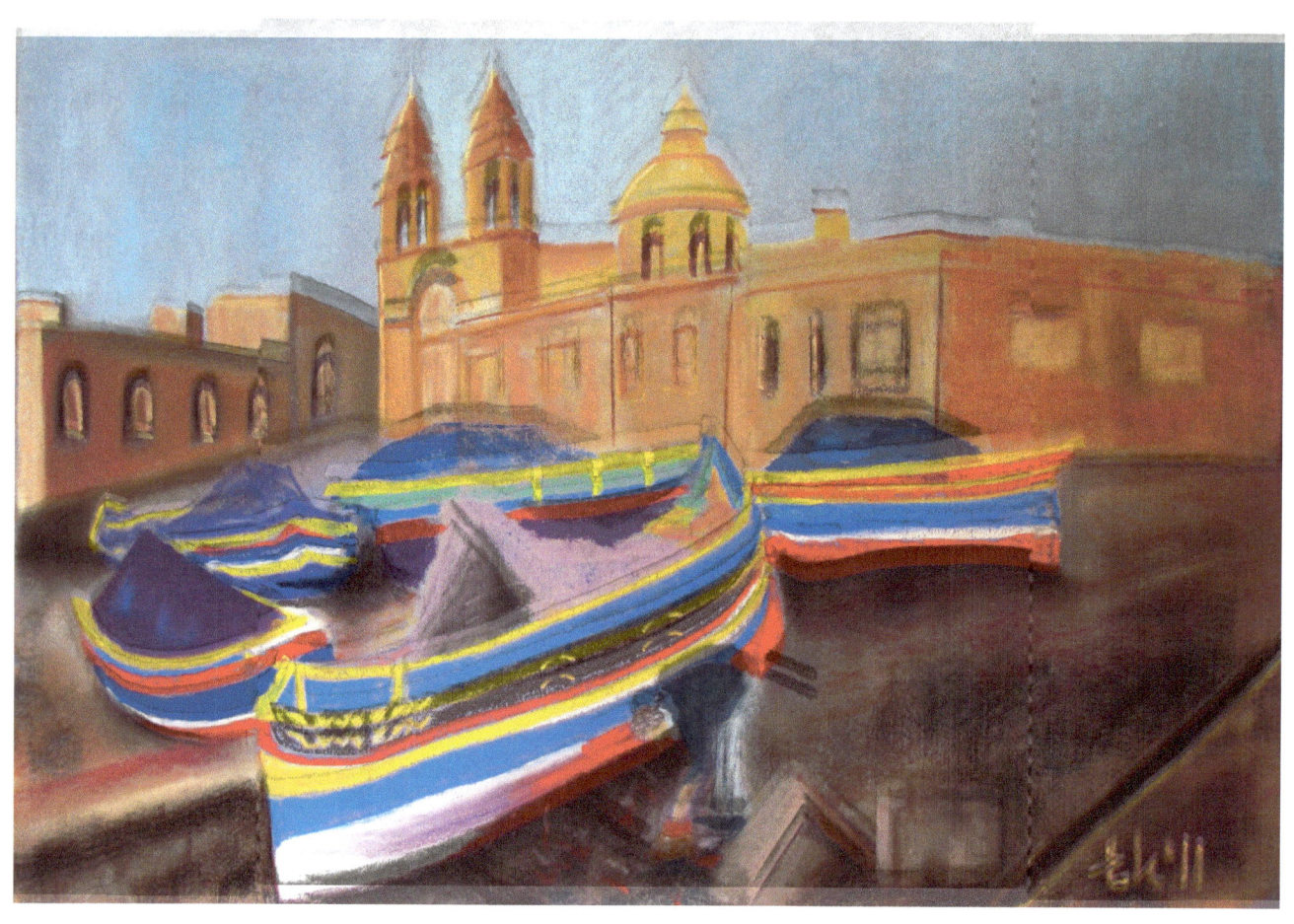

Boat painting on Malta

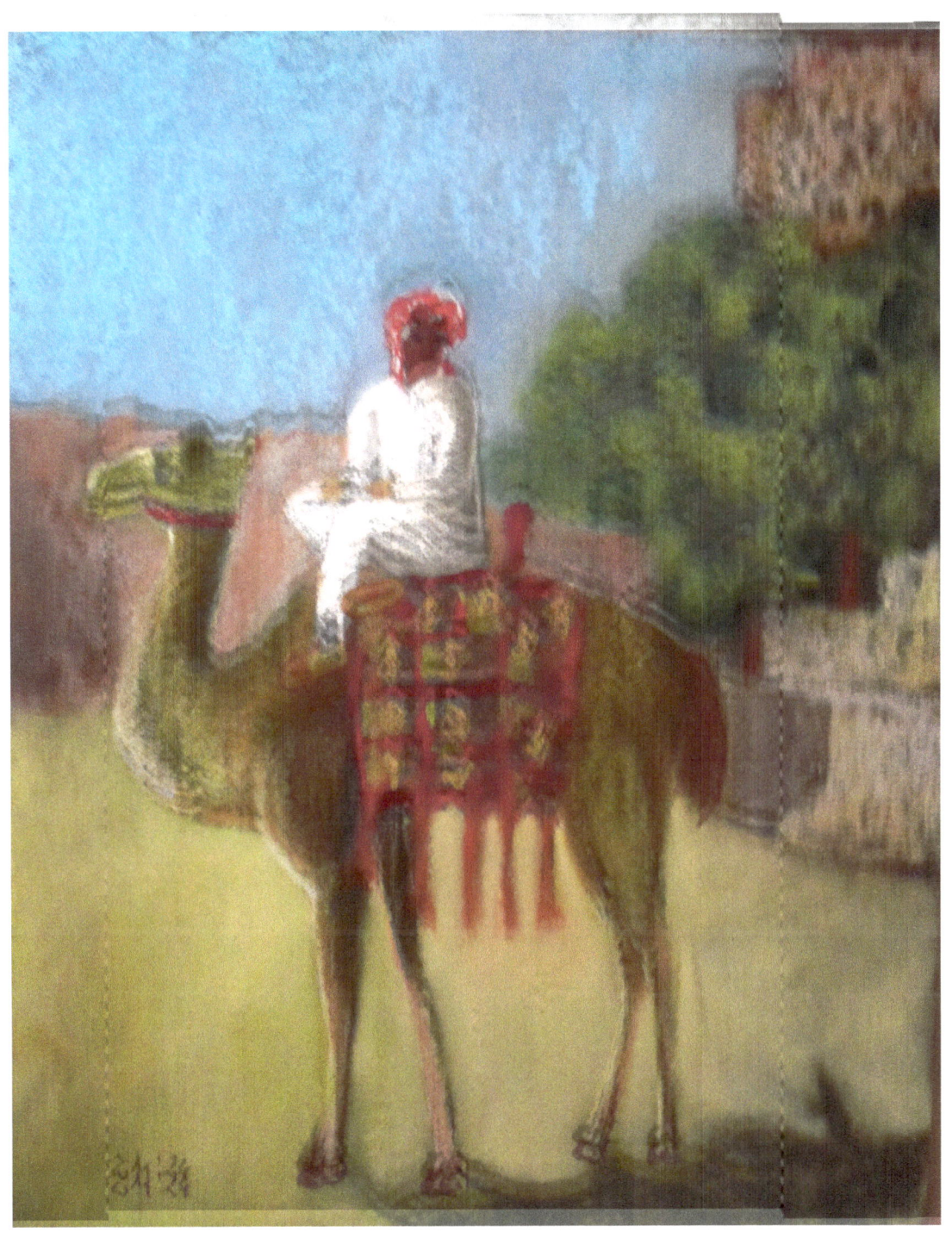

Camel driver in Petra, Jordan
Camel driver in Petra, Jordan

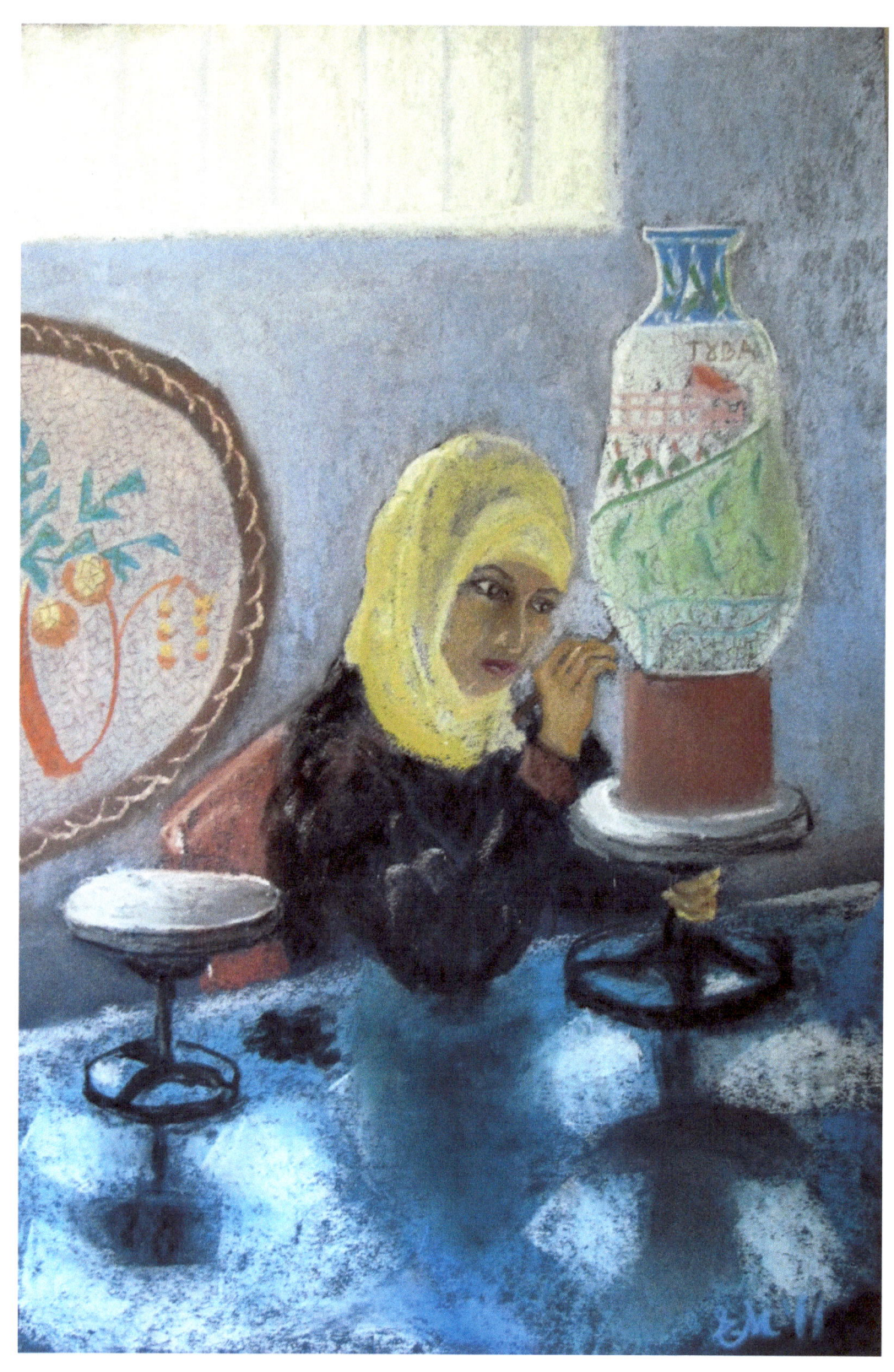

Ceramist in Madaba, Jordan

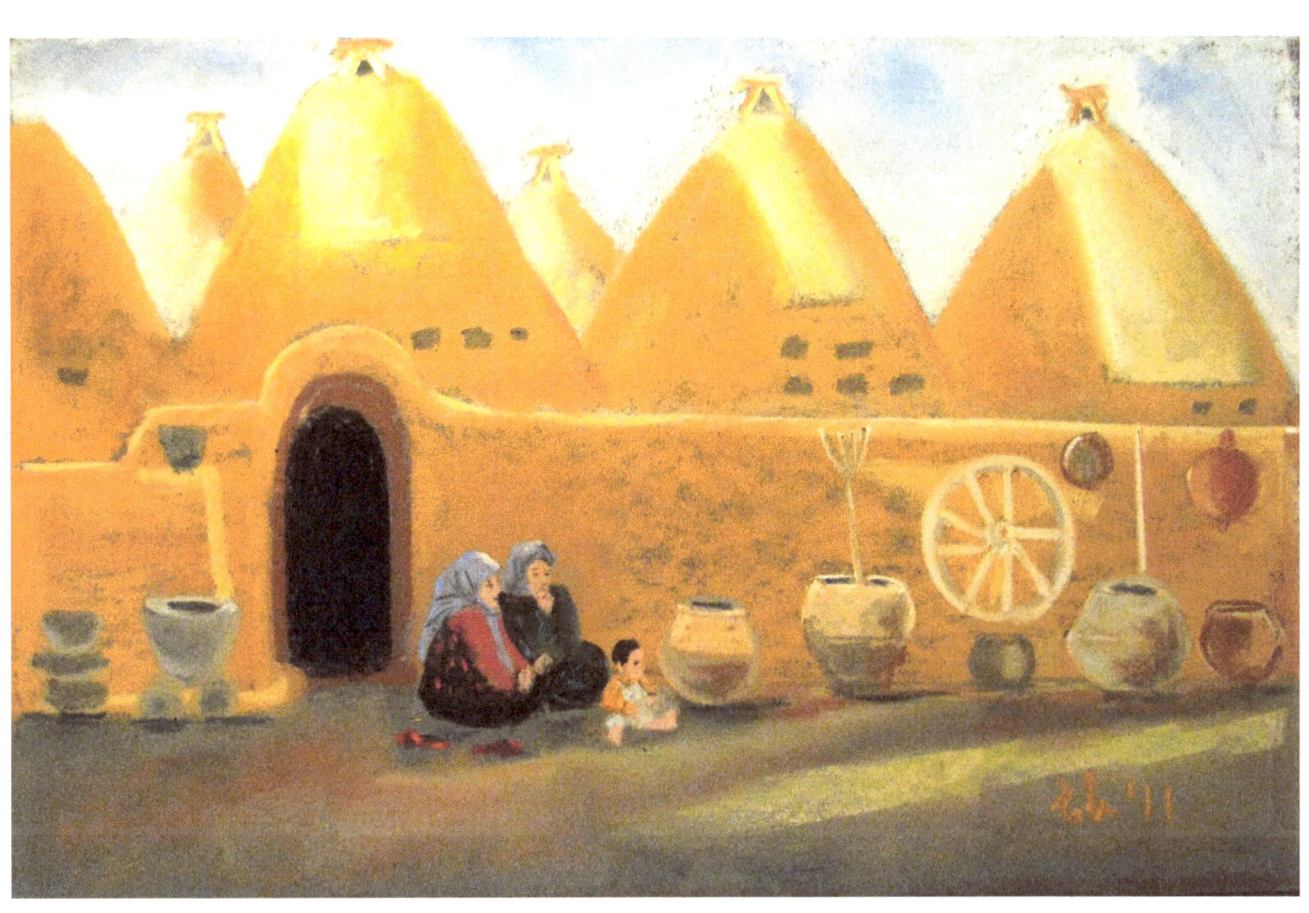

Chatting in Harran, Turkiye

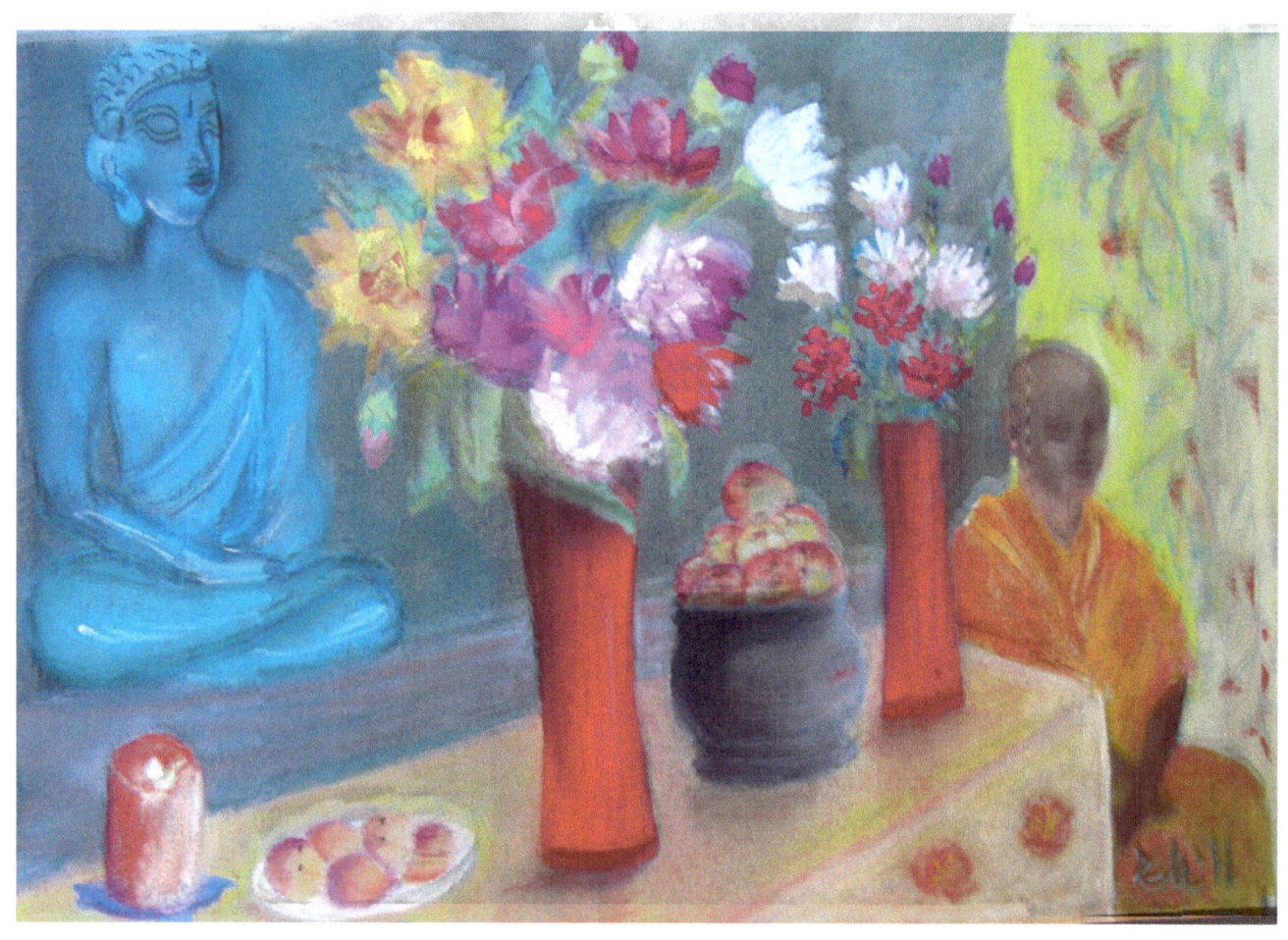

Buddhist shrine, China

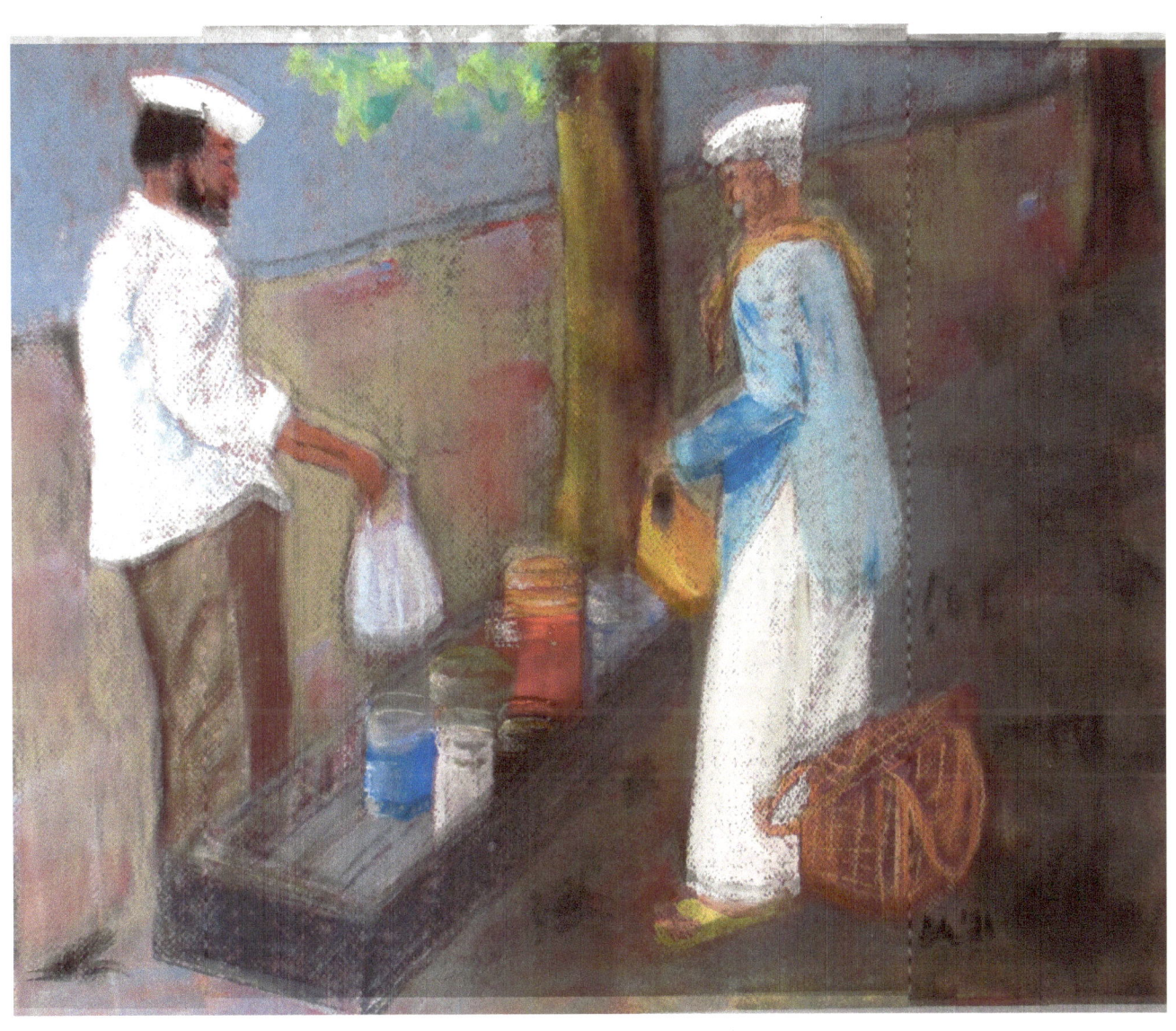

Dabawallas in Mumbai, India

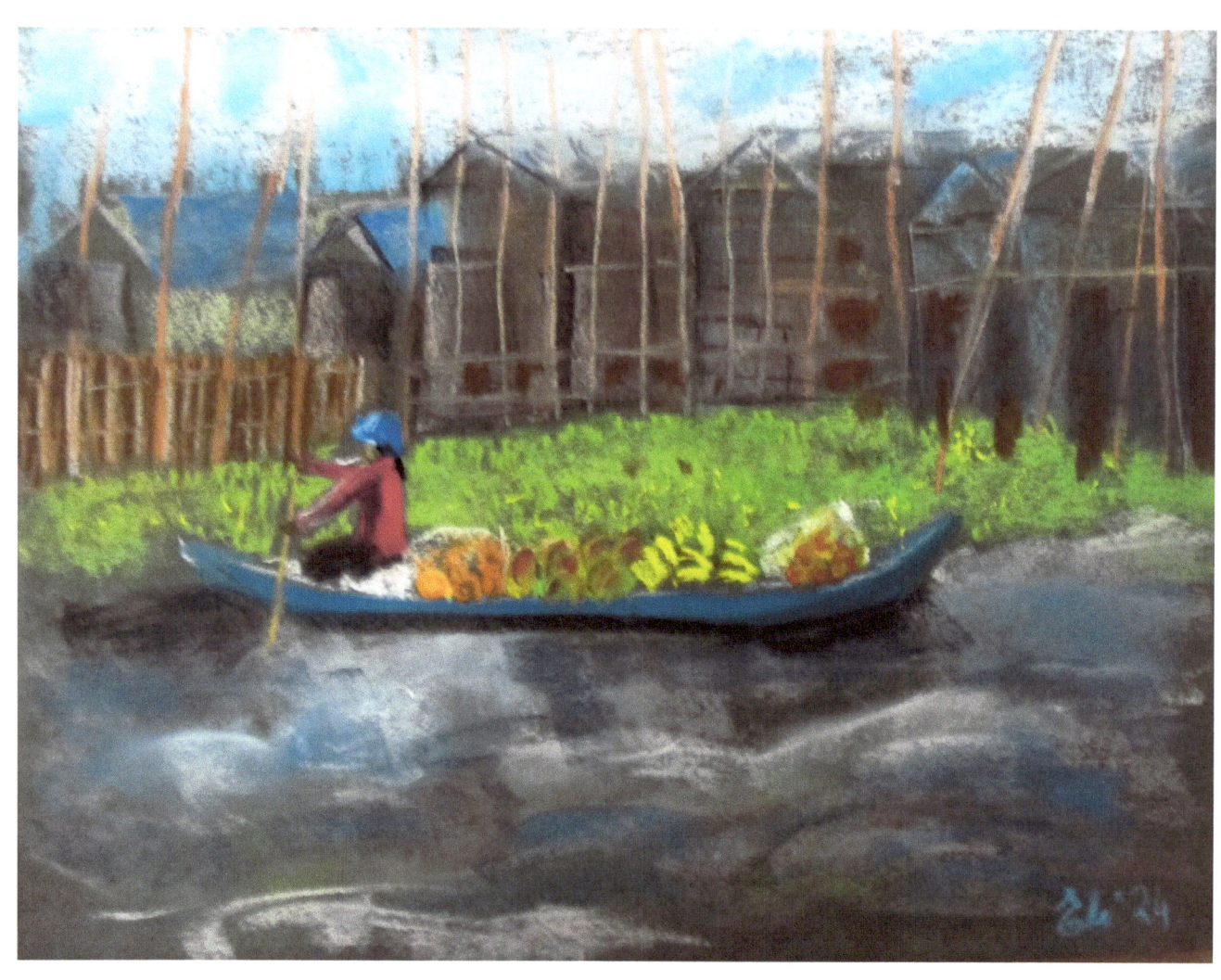

Floating village in Cambodia

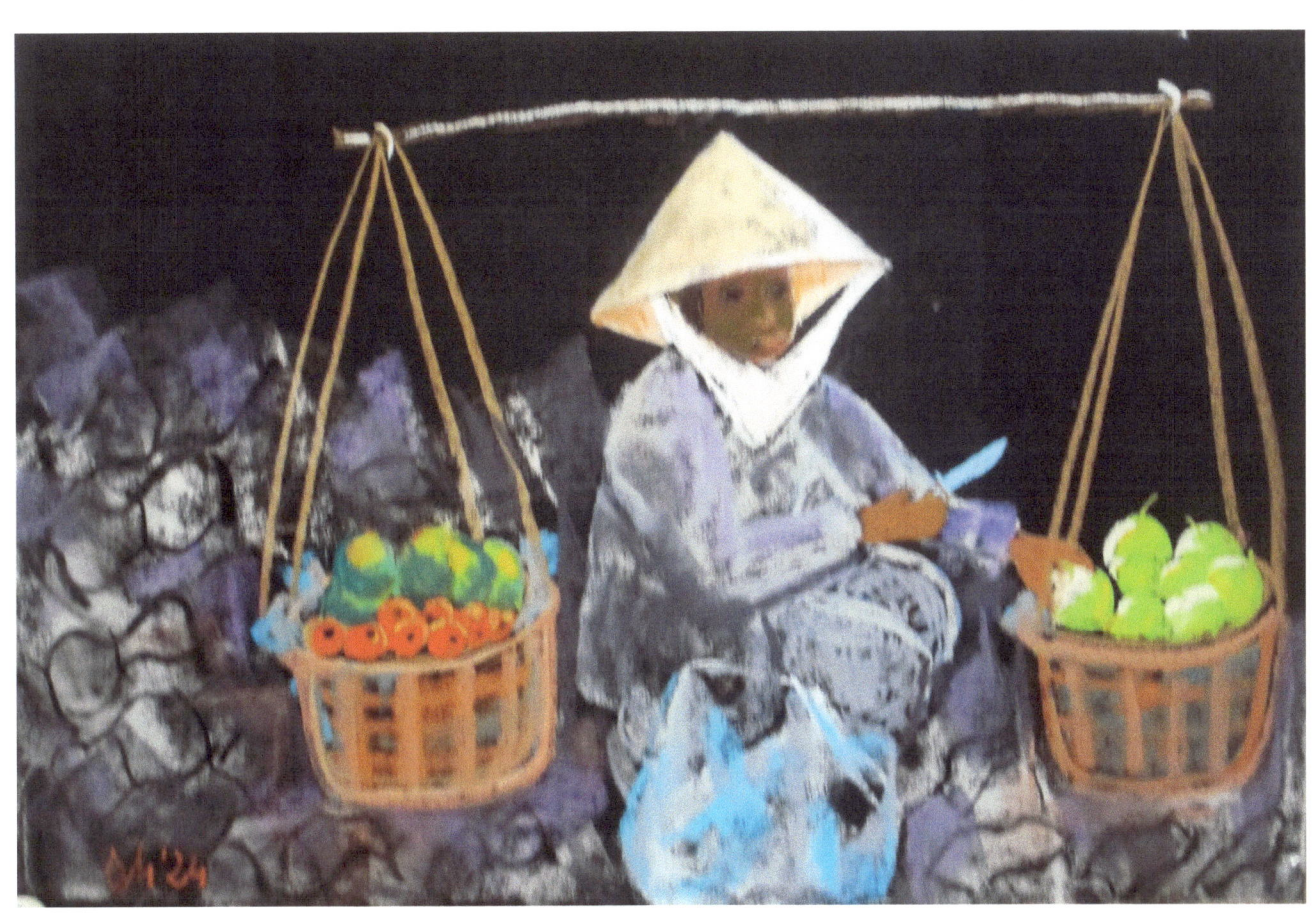

Fruit vendor, Vietnam

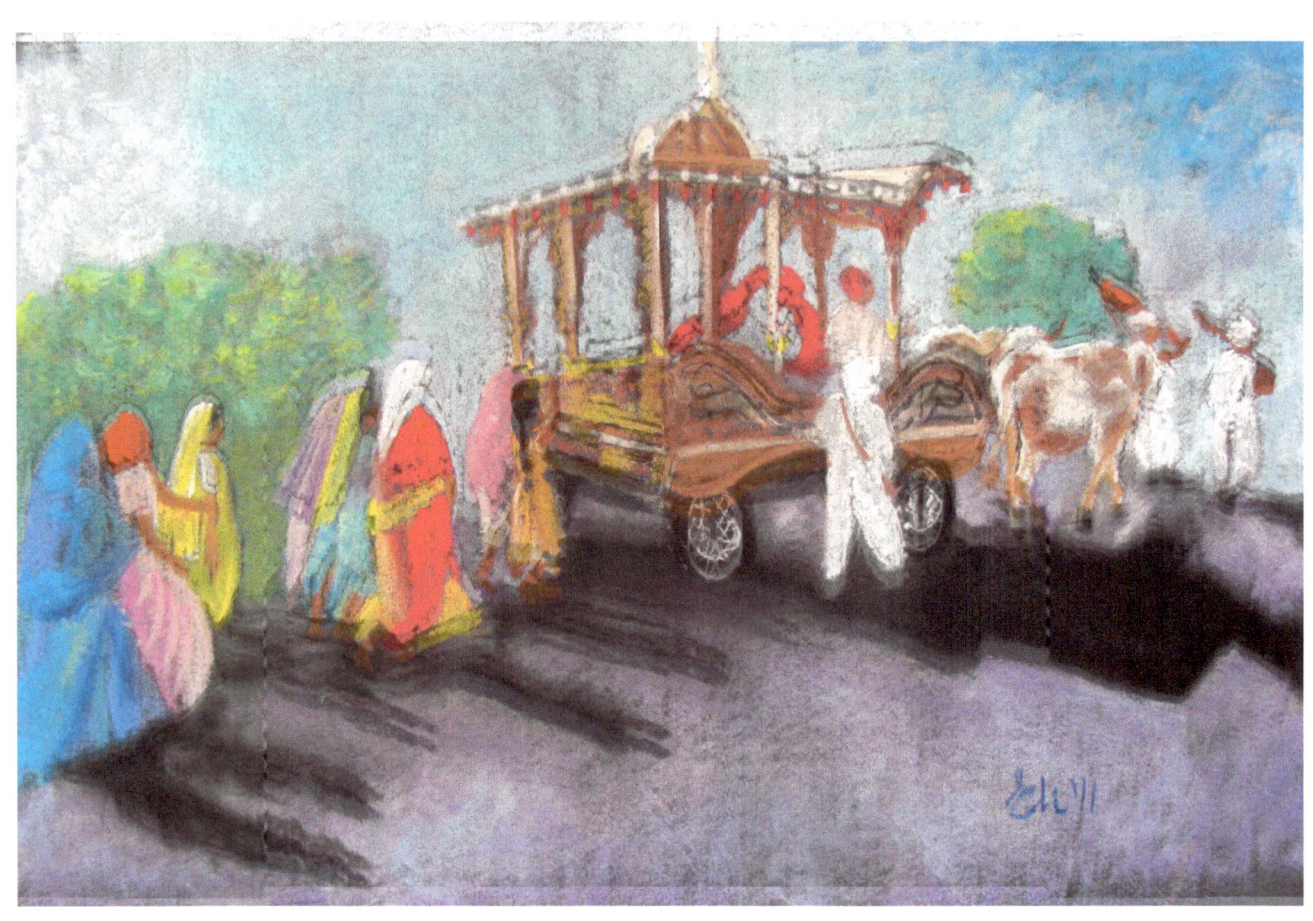

Hindu procession in rural India

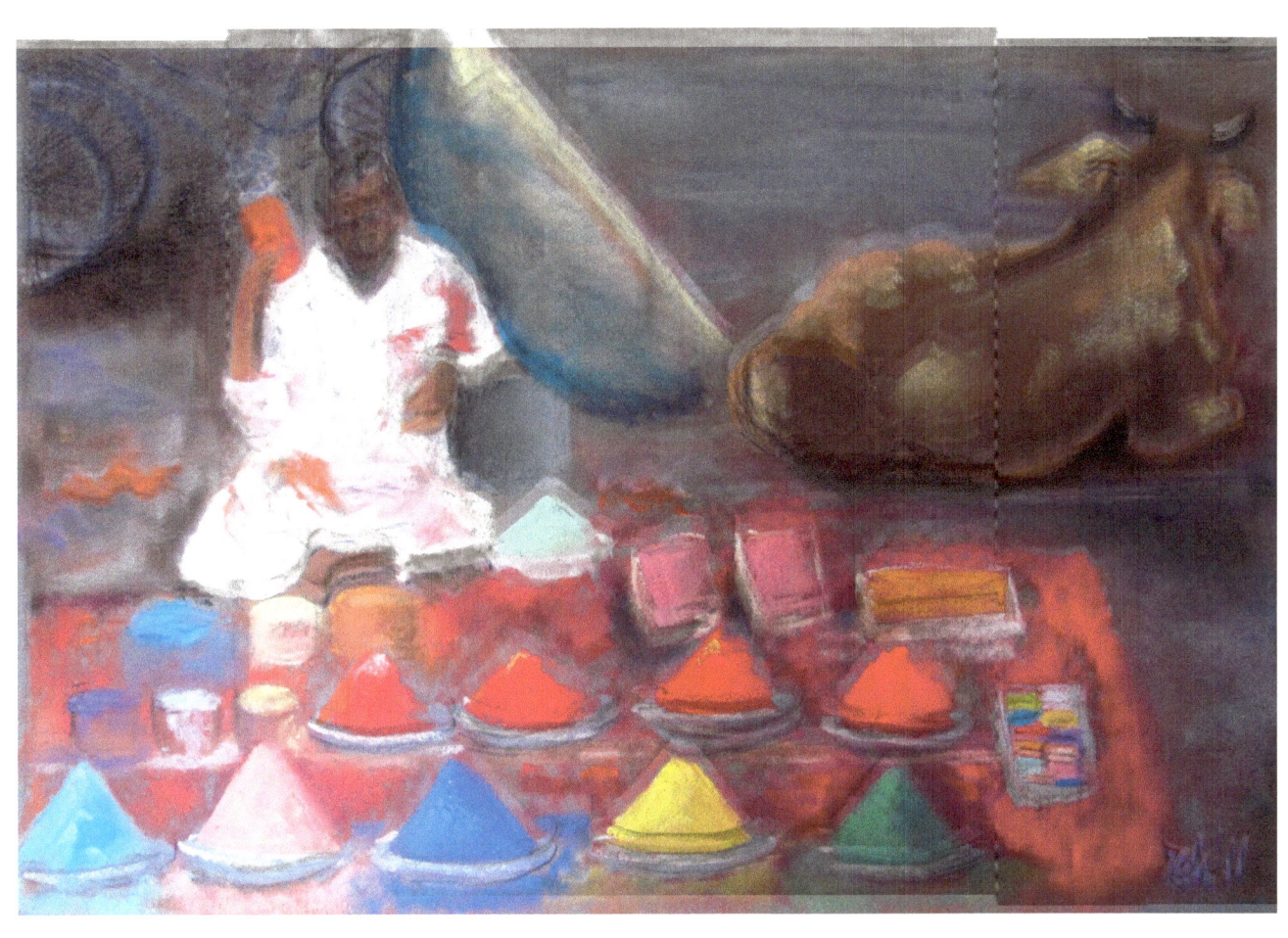

Holi powders for sale, India

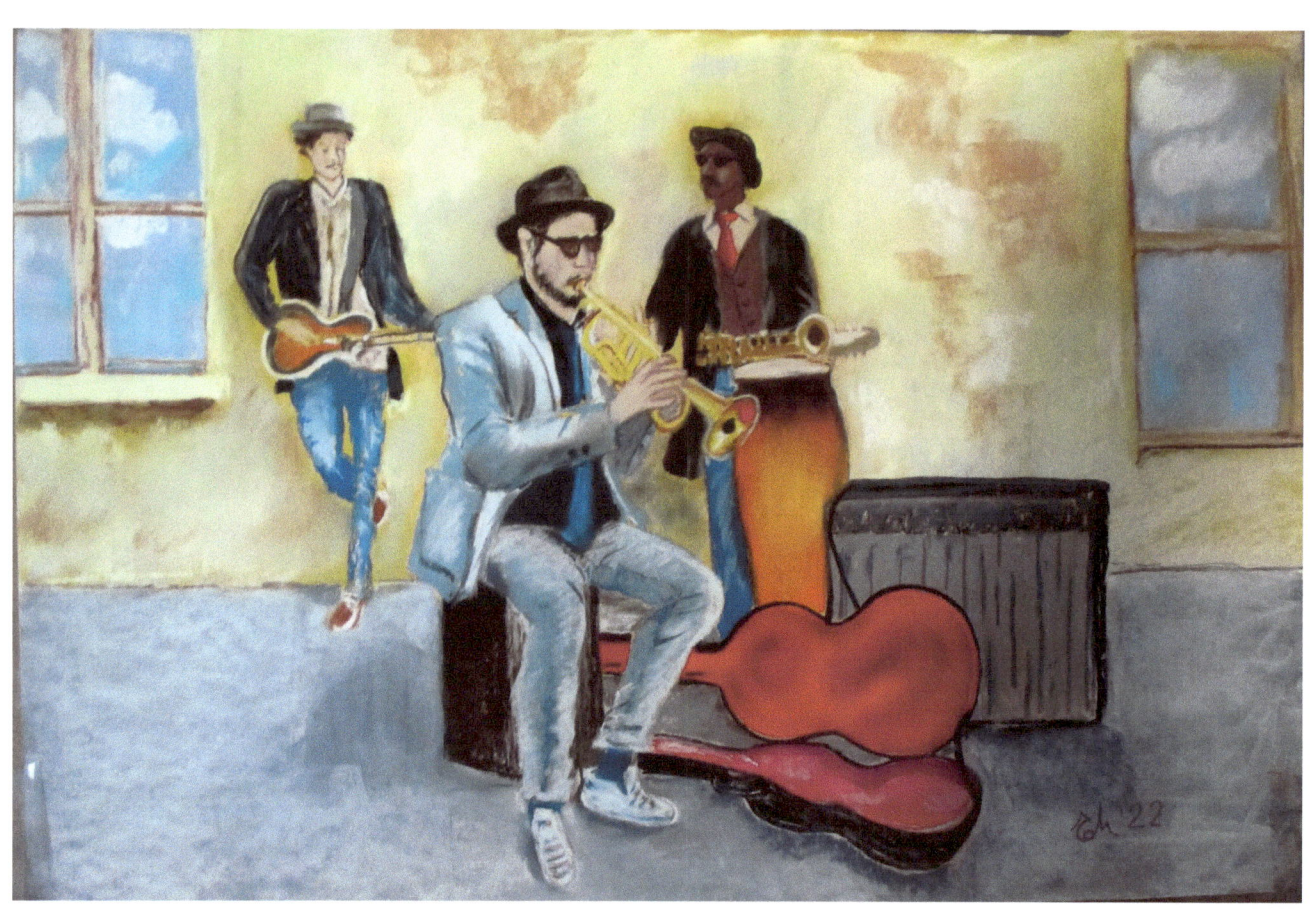

Jazz trio in a Chicago street, USA.

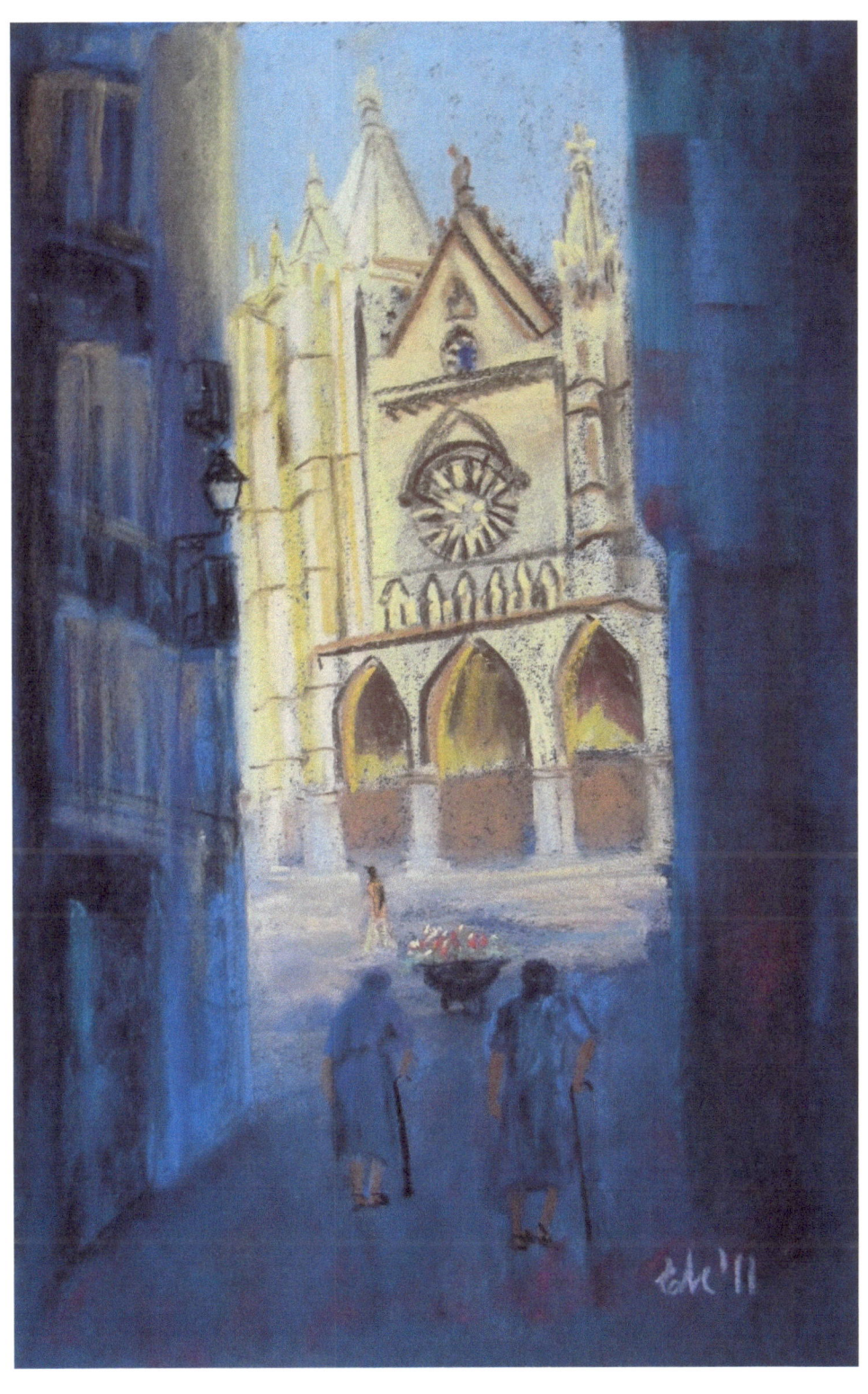

Leon, Spain

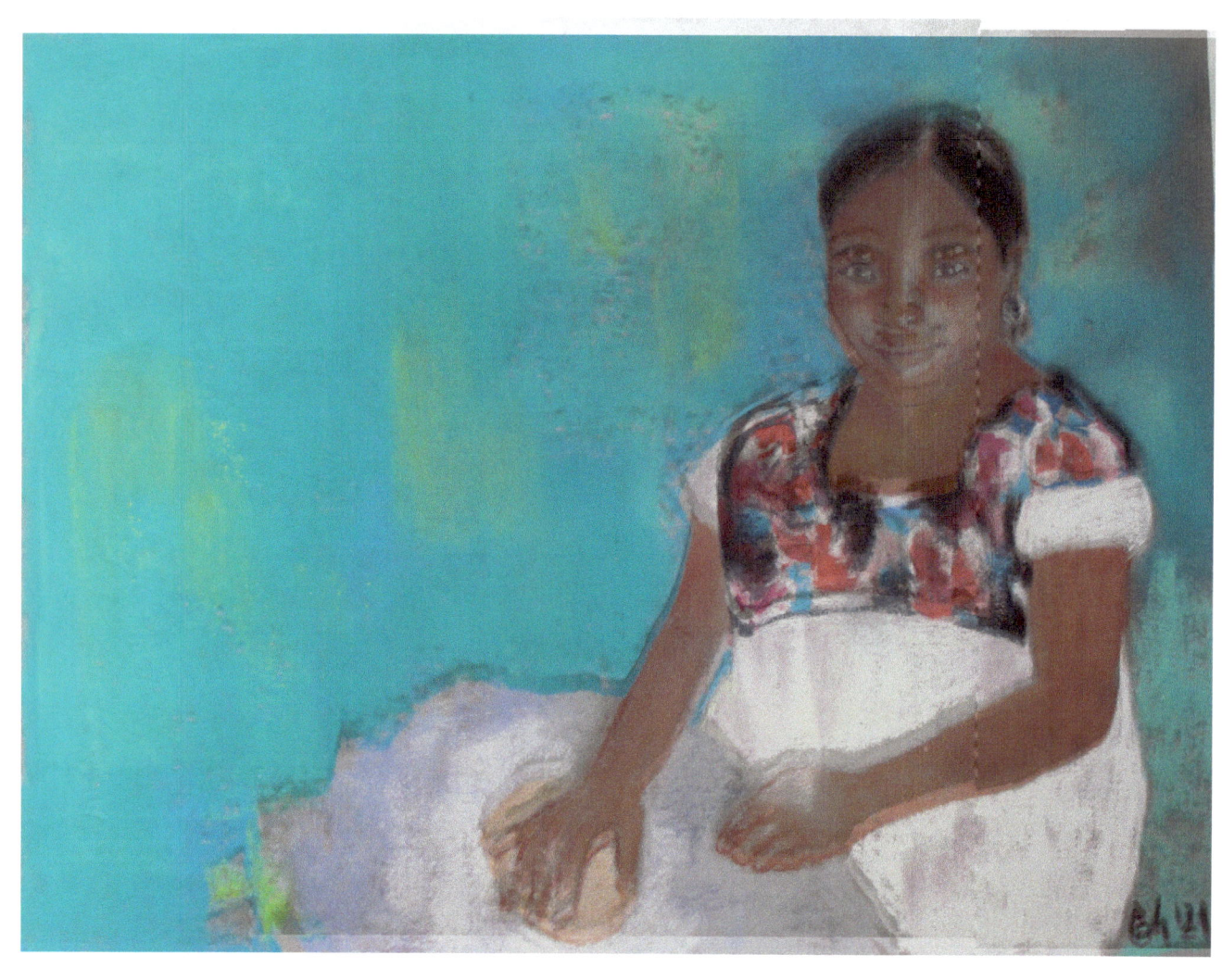

Making tacos at Chichenitza, Mexico
Making tacos at Chichenitza, Mexico

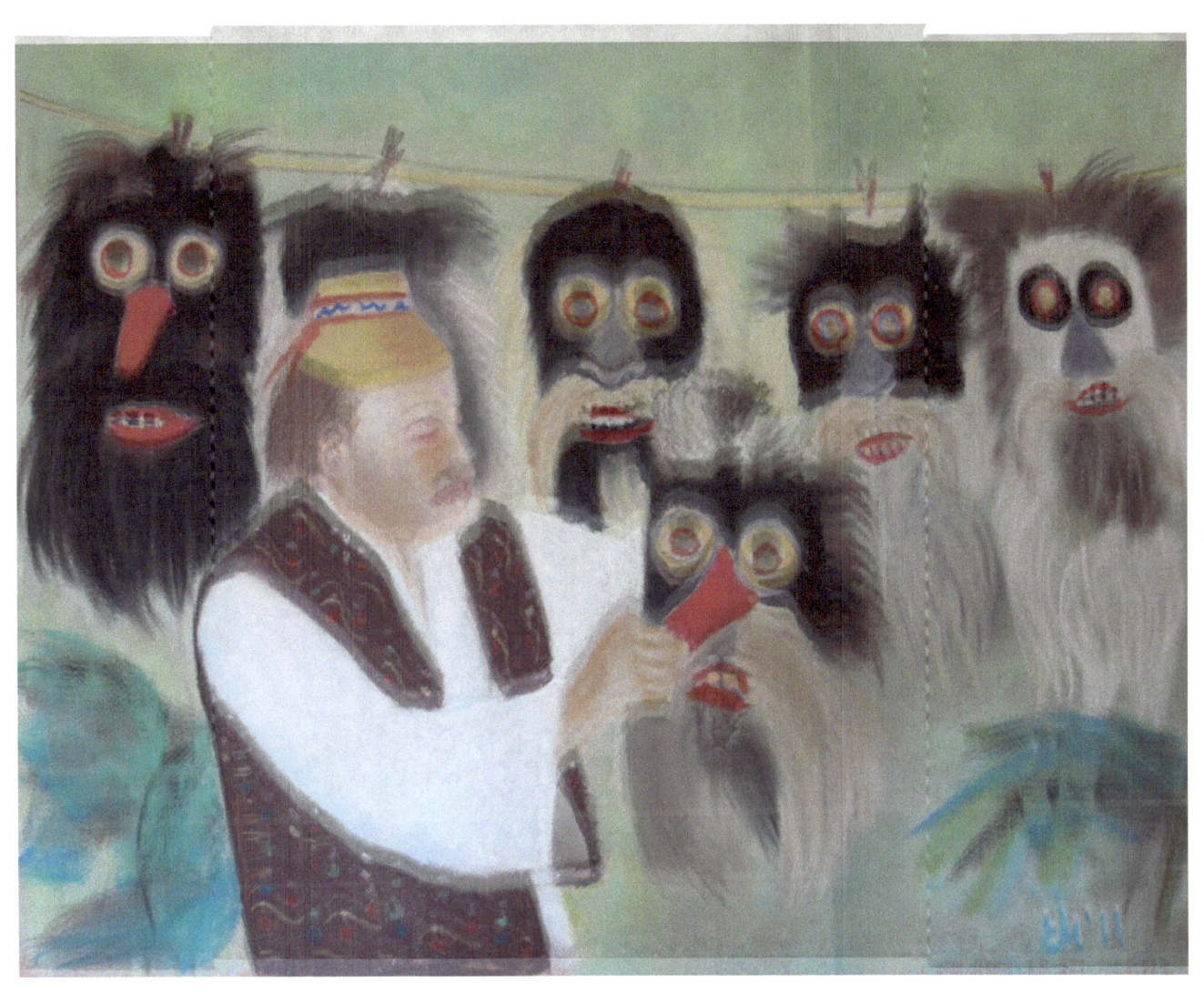

Maskmaker in Maramures, Romania
Maskmaker in Maramures, Romania

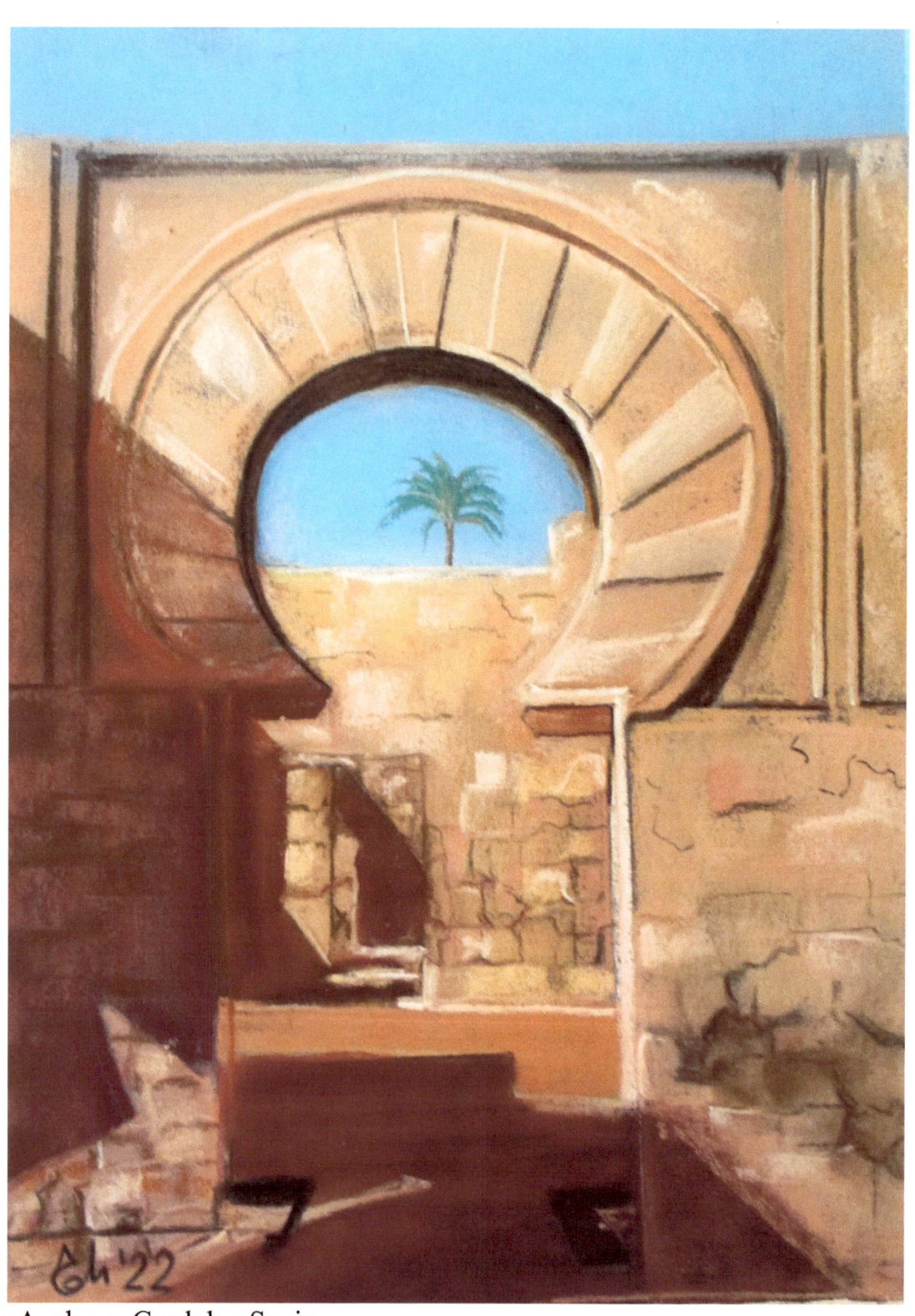

Medina Azahara, Cordoba, Spain

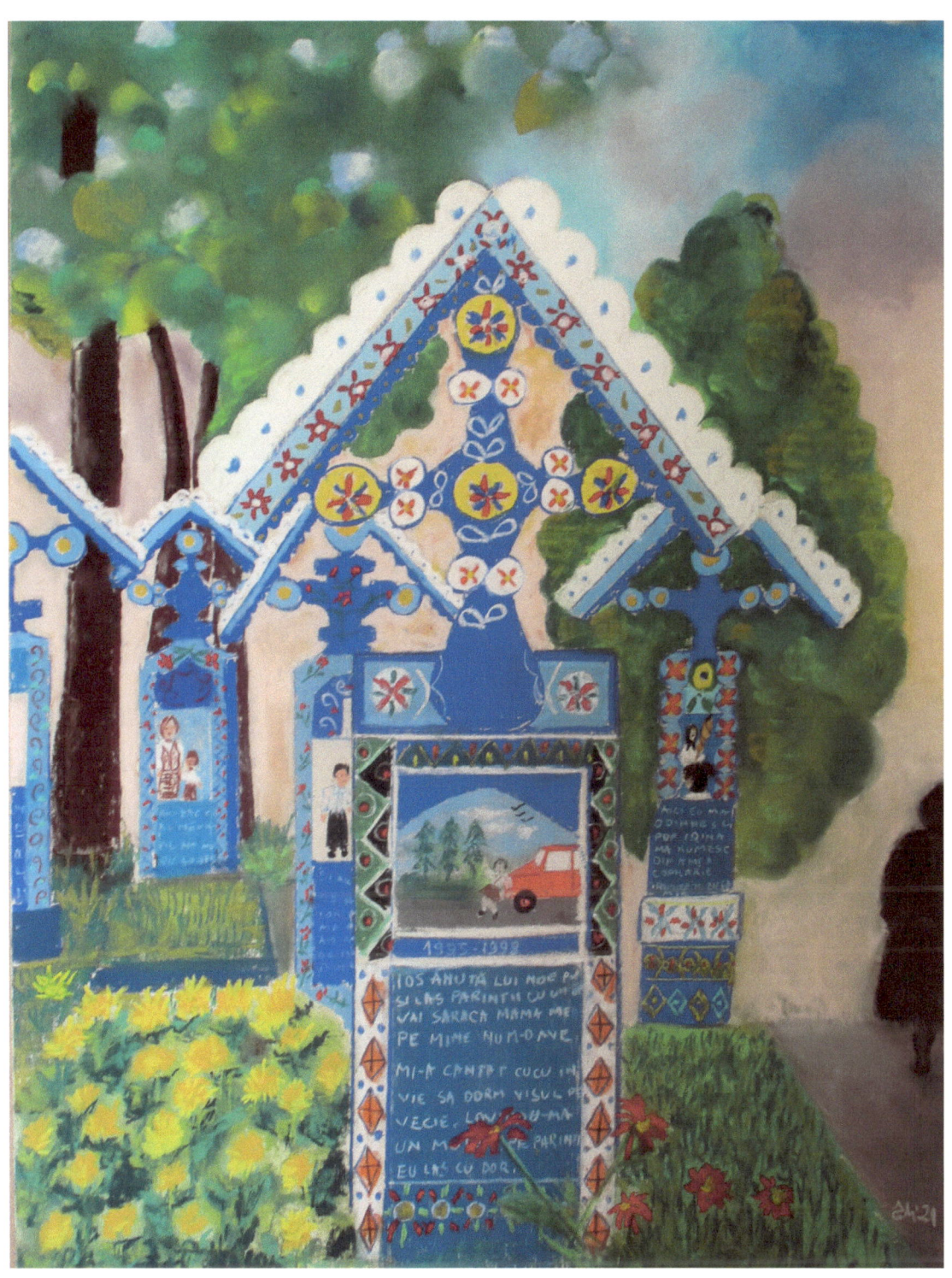

The Merry Cemetery at Sapanta, Romania

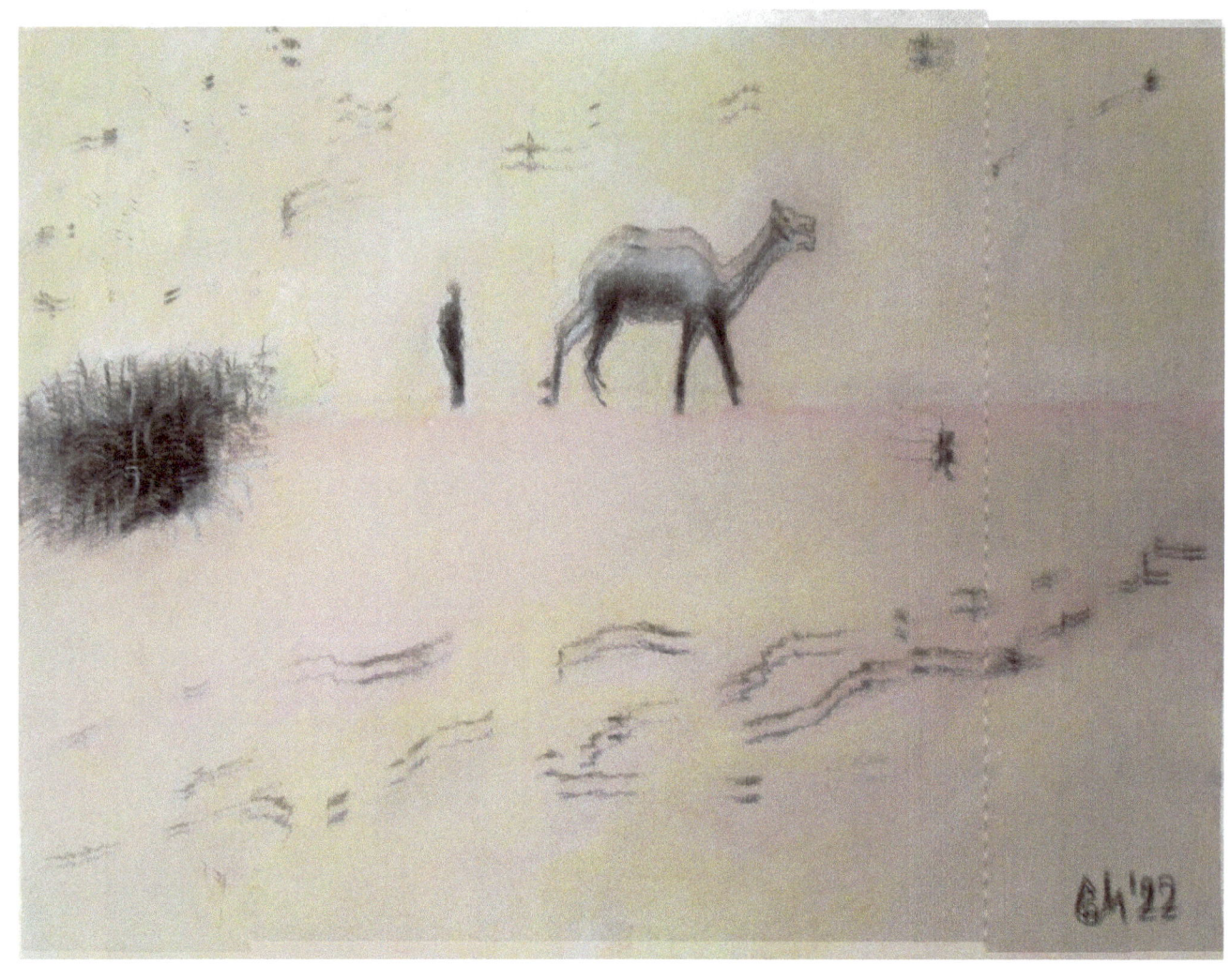

Near Assuan, Egypt

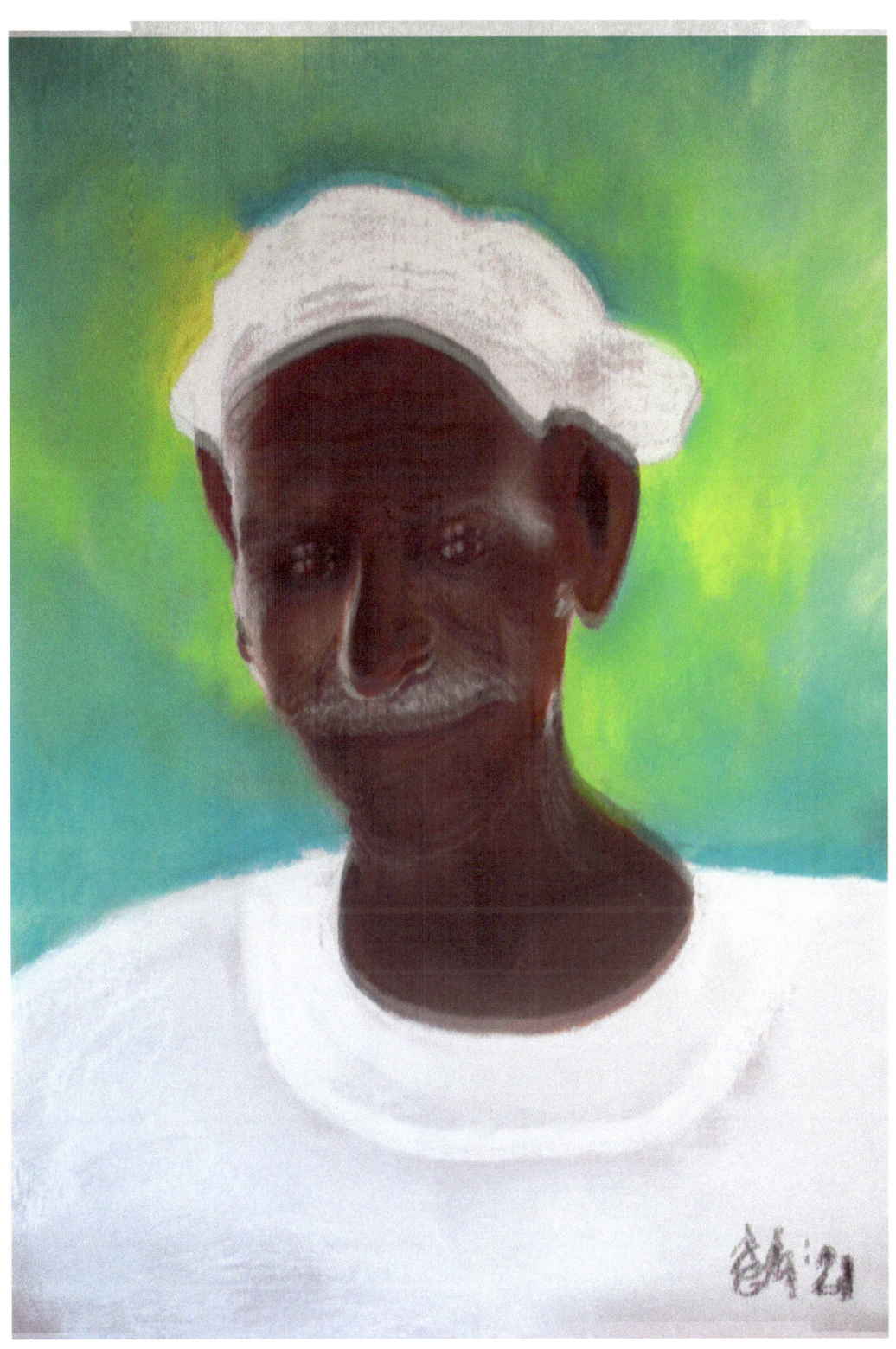

Nubian Boatman, Egypt
Nubian Boatman, Egypt

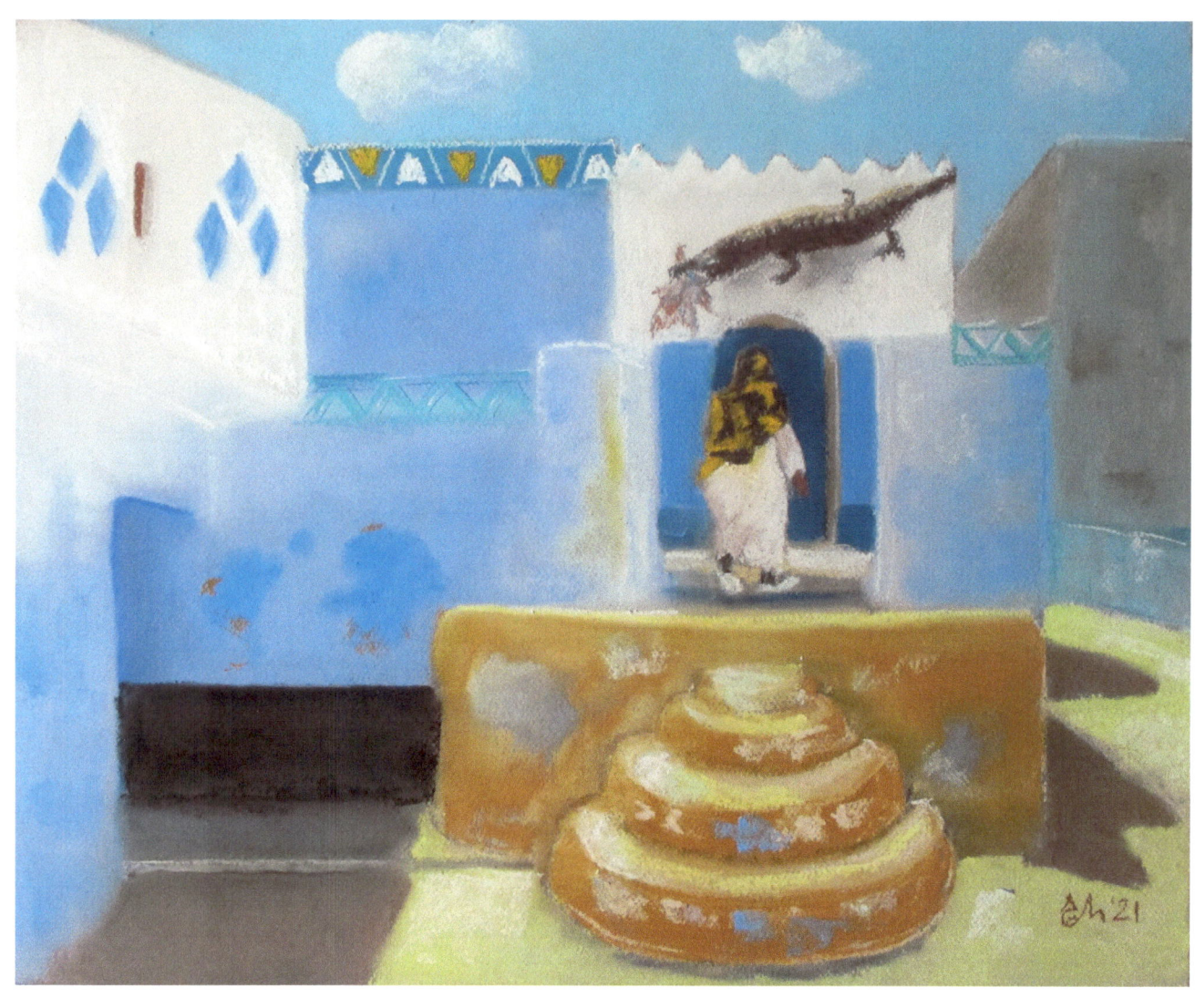

Nubian village house, Egypt

Nubian village woman, Egypt

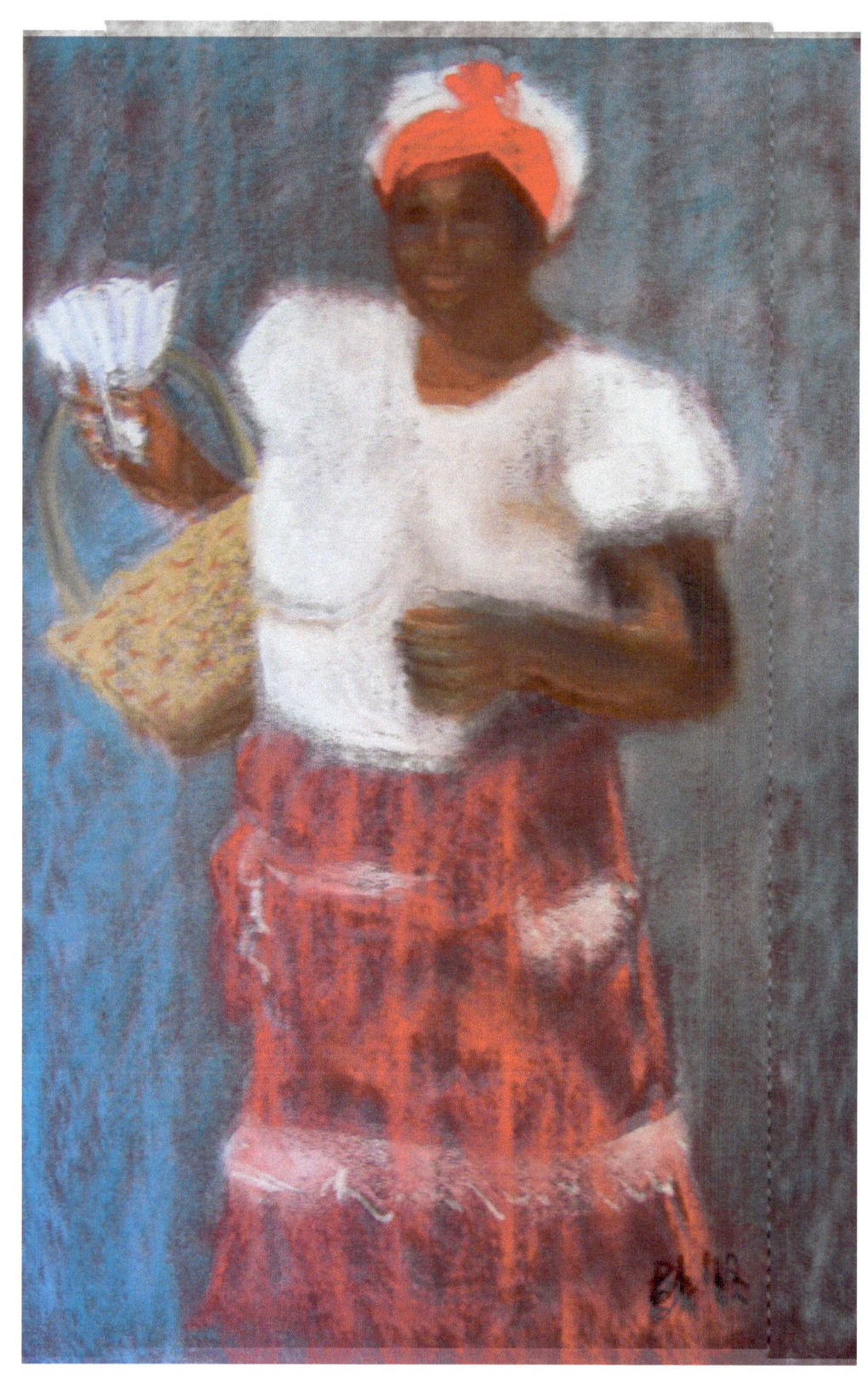

Peanut seller, Havana, Cuba
Peanut seller, Havana, Cuba

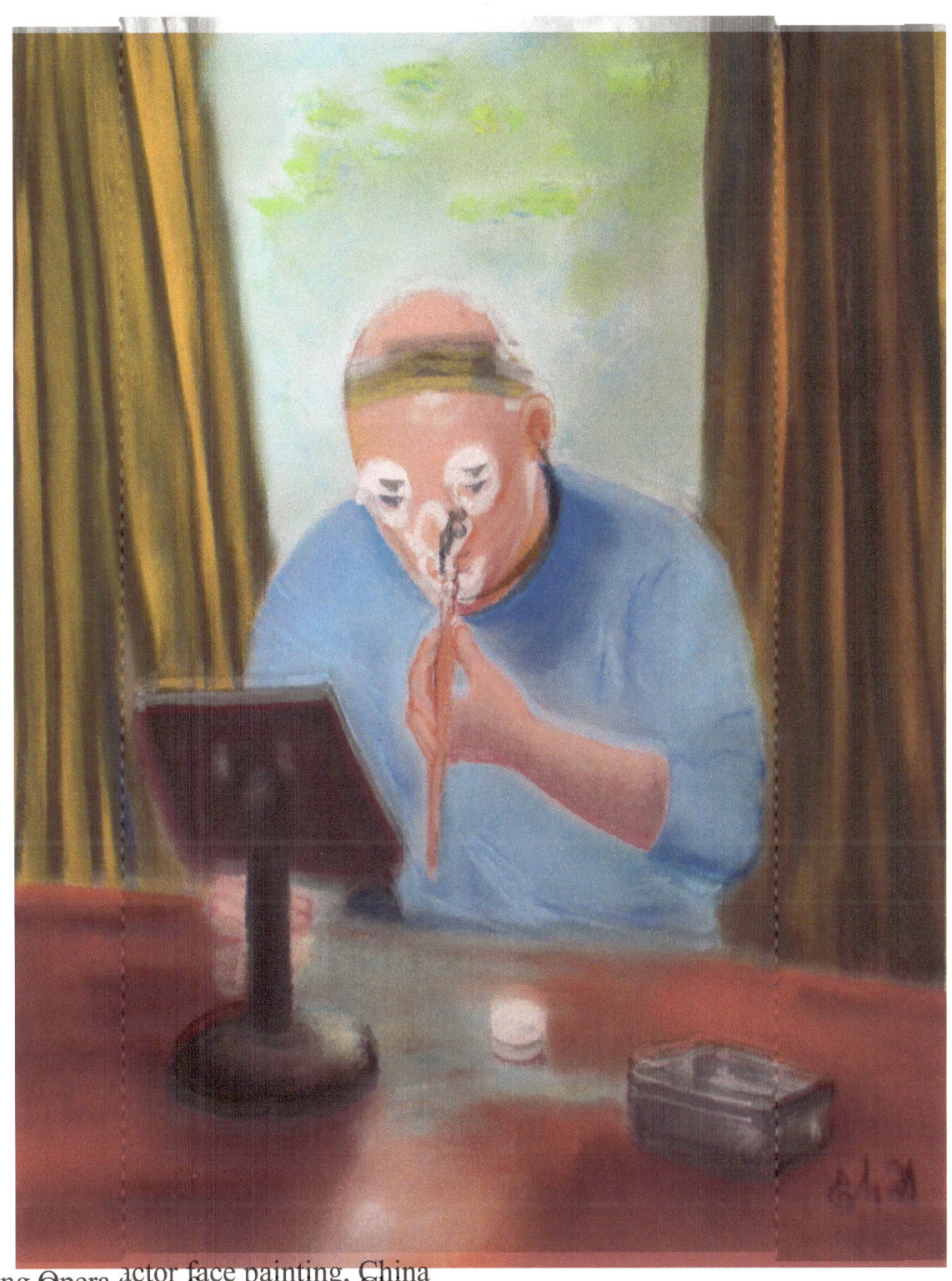

Peking Opera actor face painting, China
Peking Opera actor face painting, China

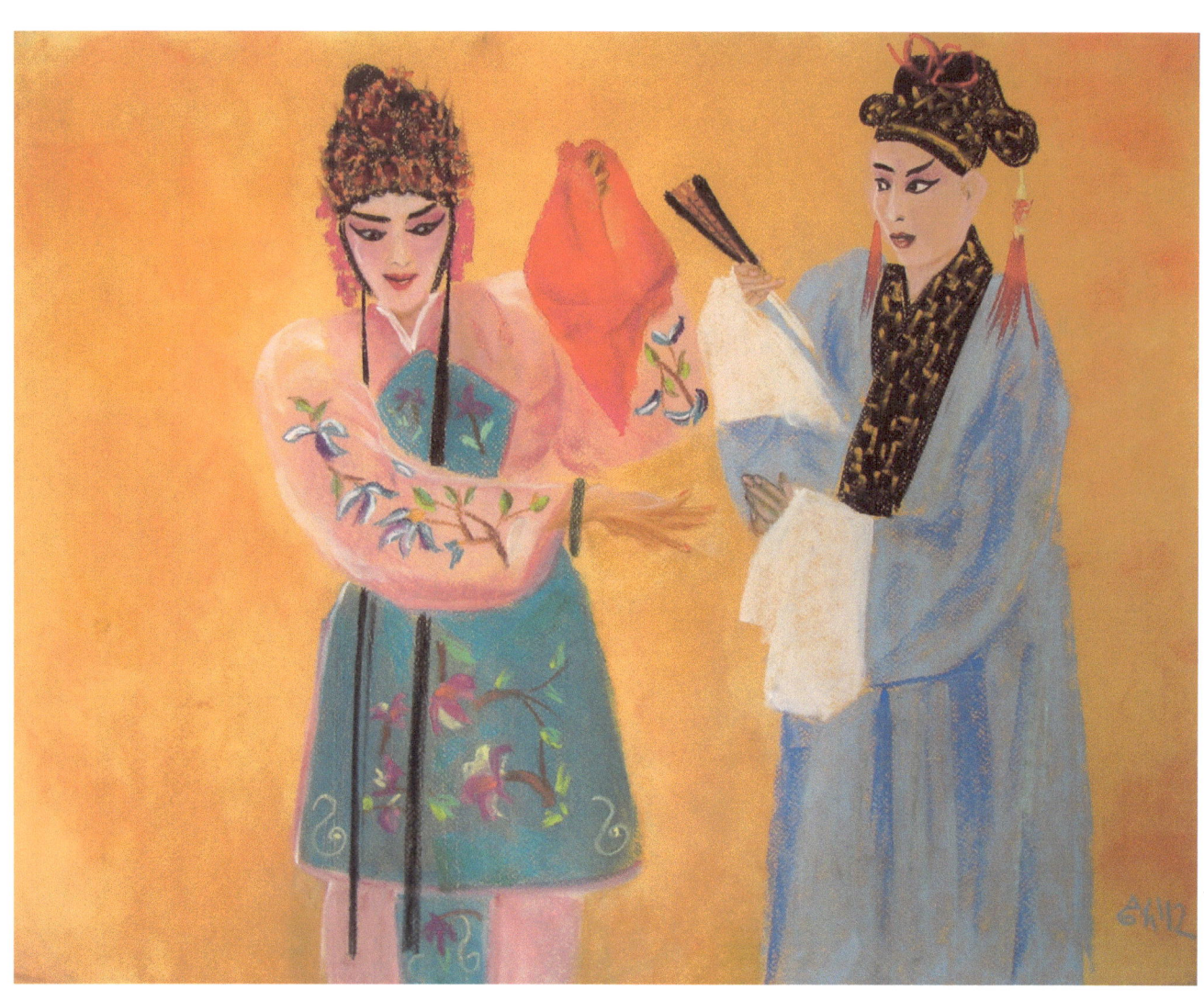

Peking Opera performance, China

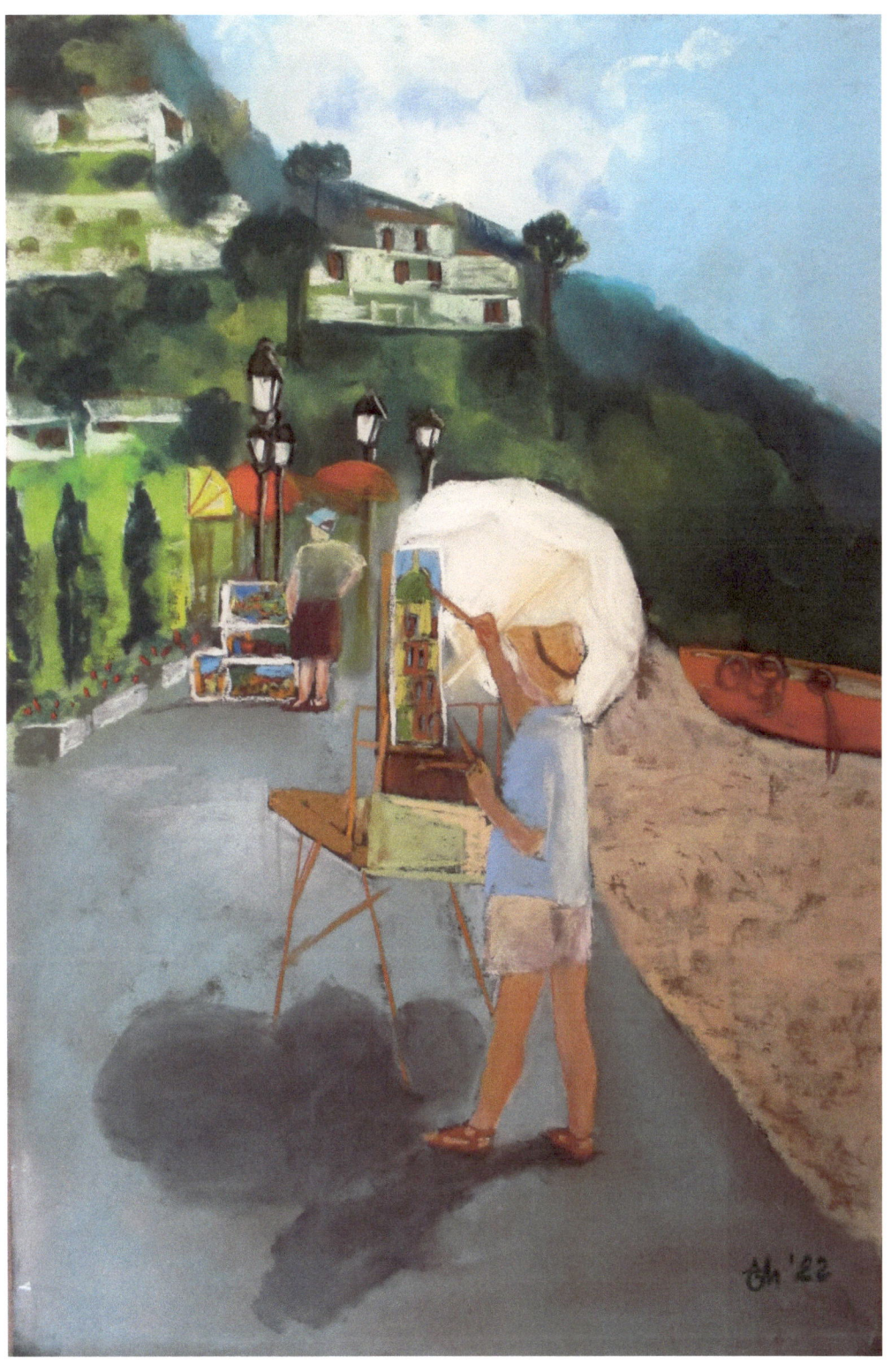

Positano street artist, Italy

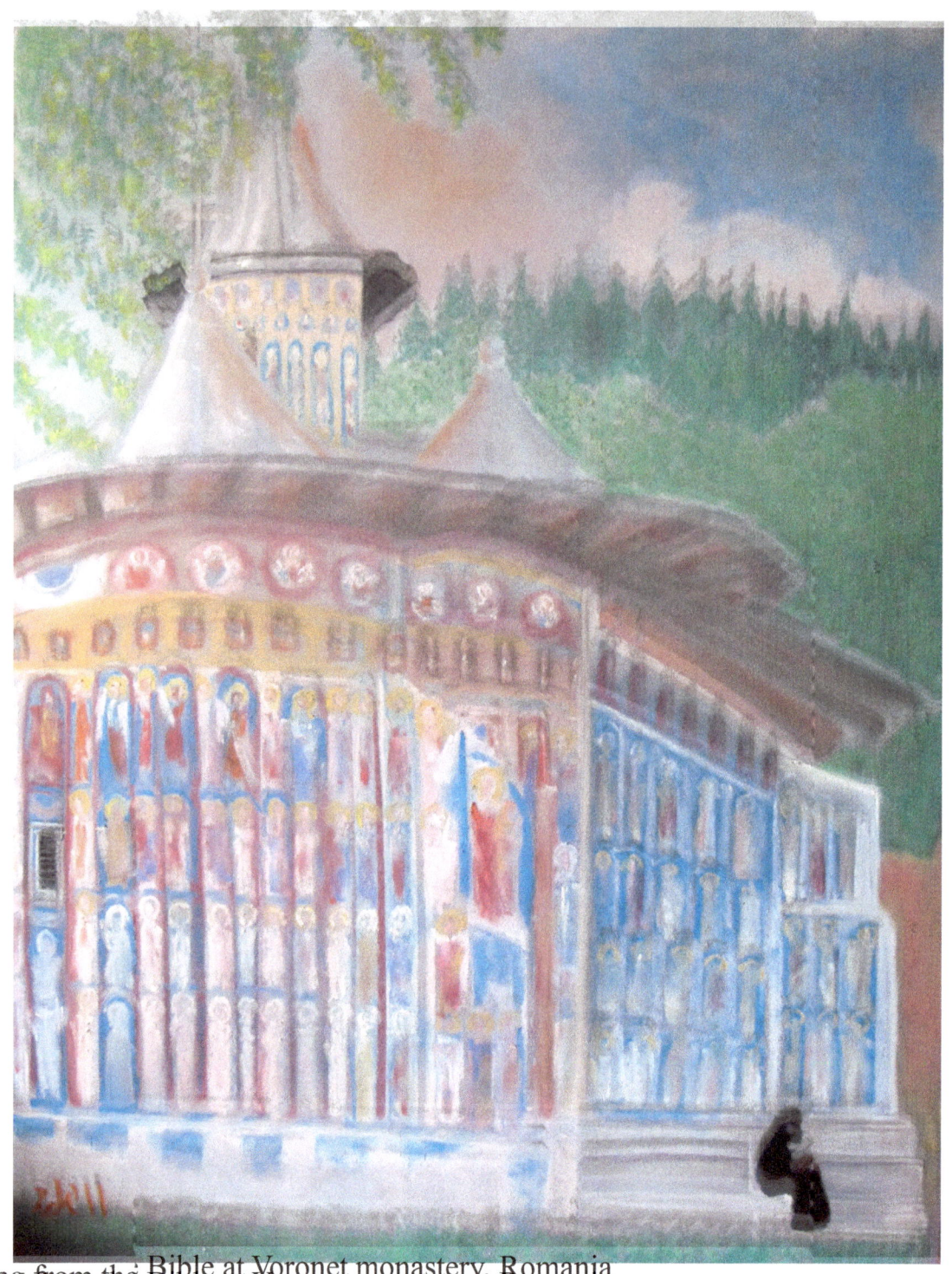

Reading from the Bible at Voronet monastery, Romania
Reading from the Bible at Voronet monastery, Romania

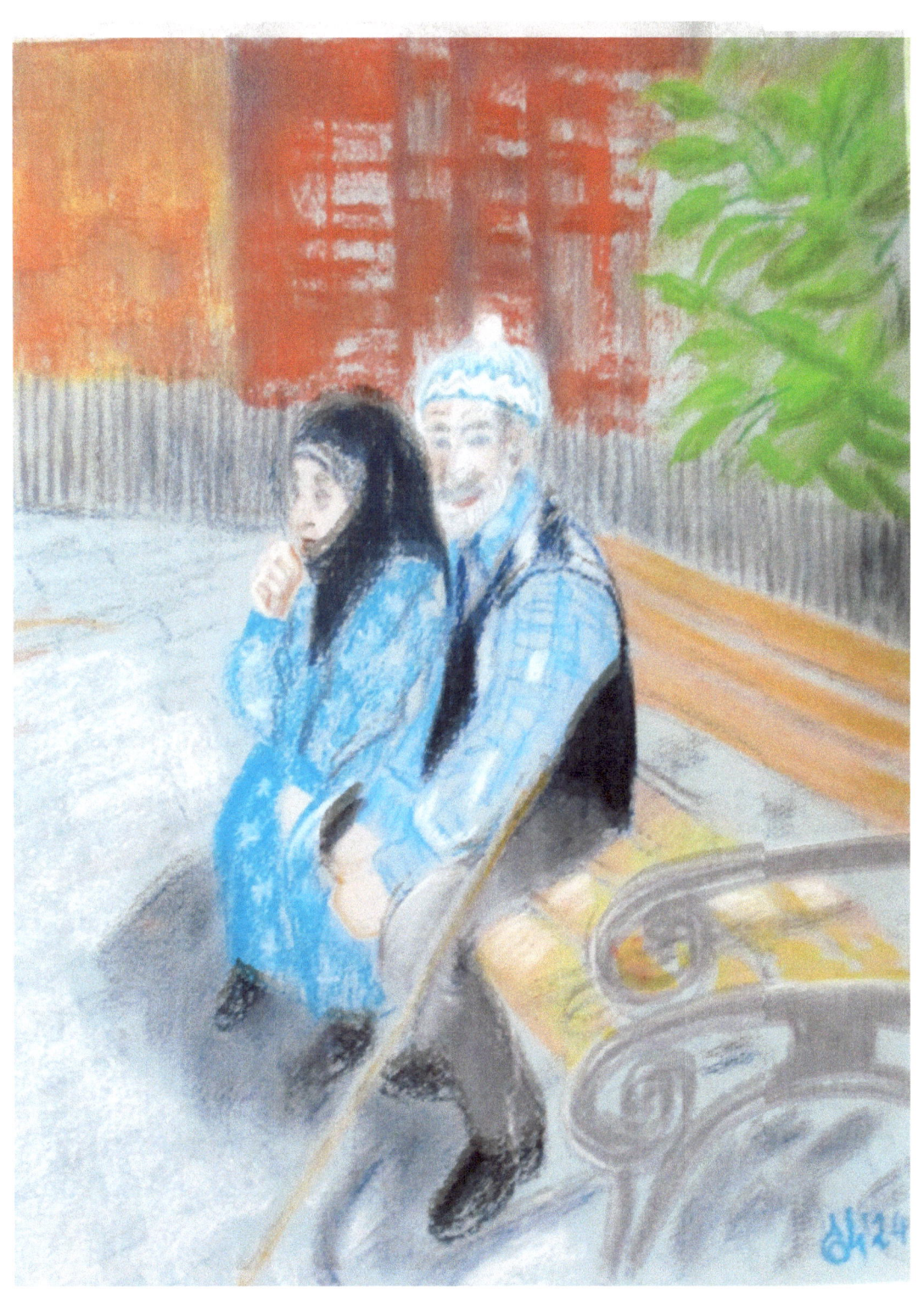

Resting at Galata Tower, Istanbul, Turkiye
Resting at Galata Tower, Istanbul, Turkiye

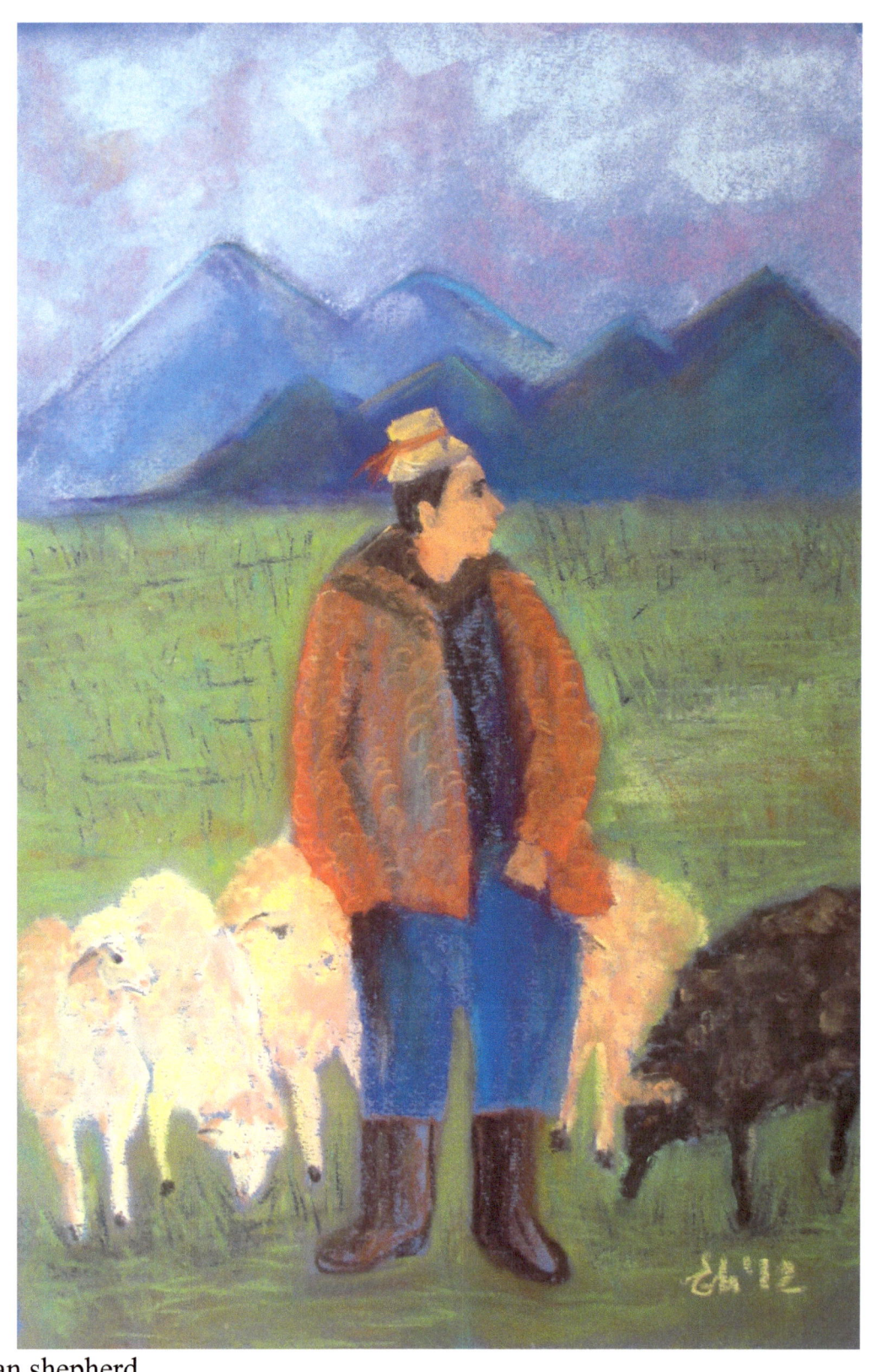

Romanian shepherd

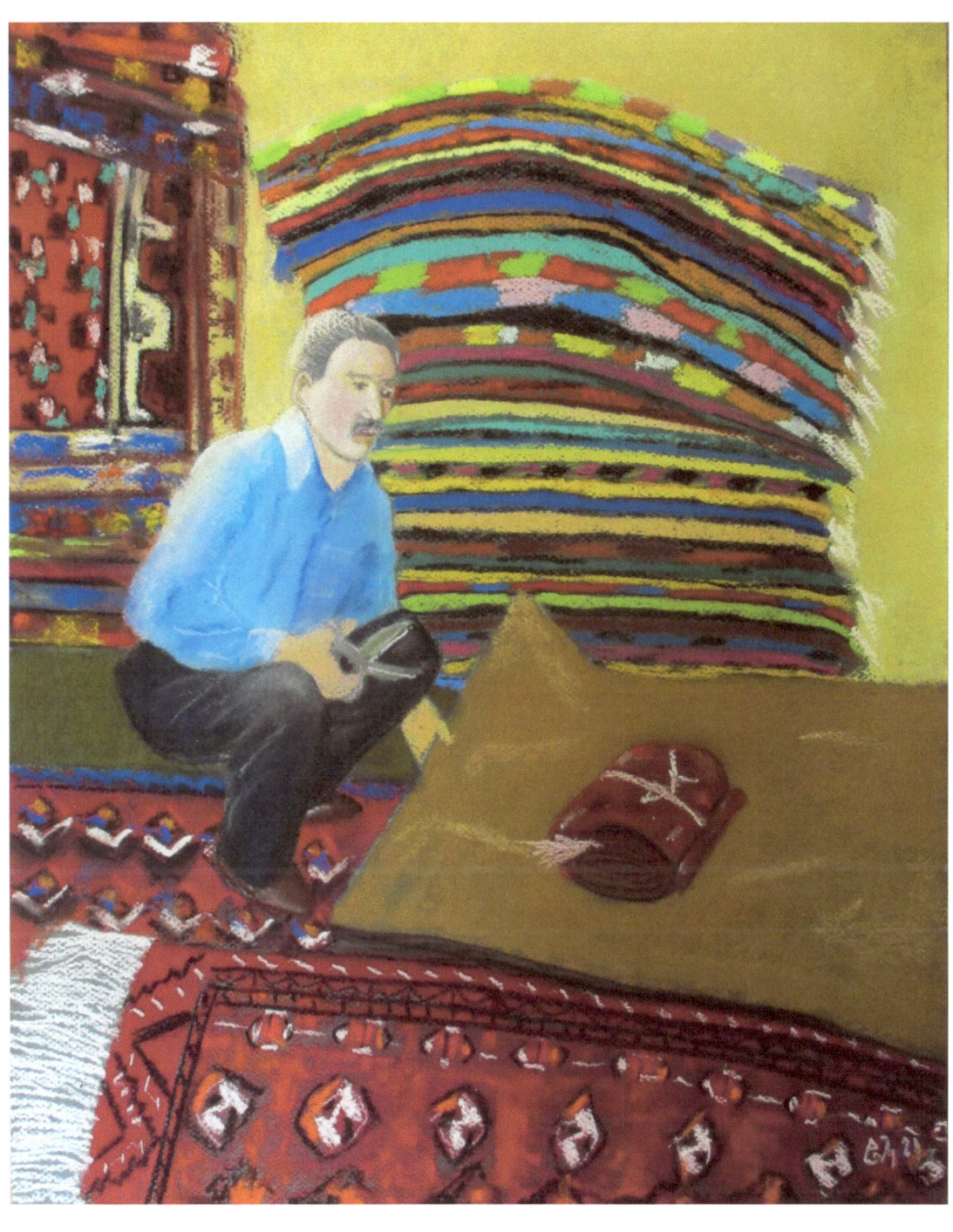

Rug seller in the Grand bazaar, Istanbul, Turkiye

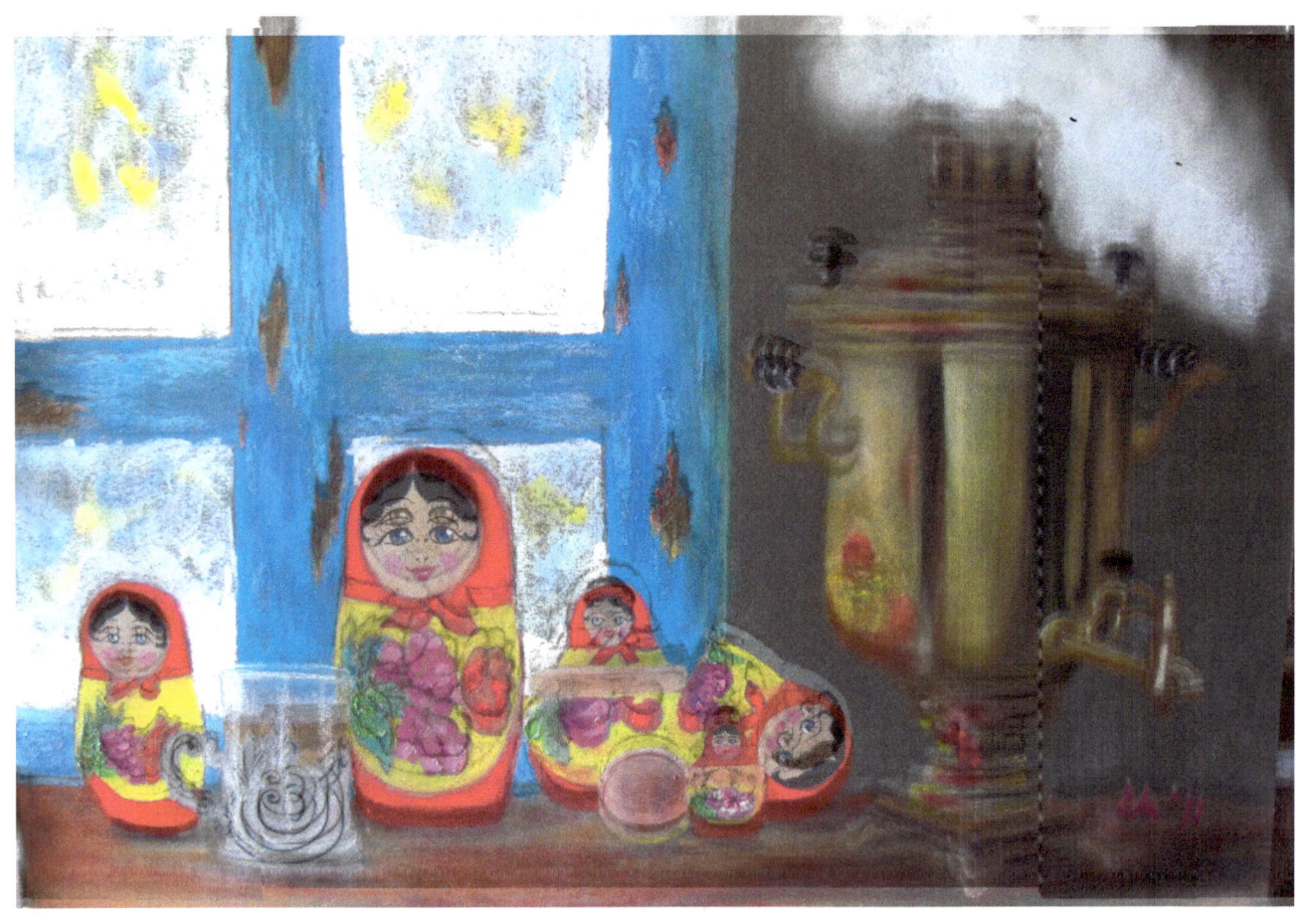

Russian Tea Time

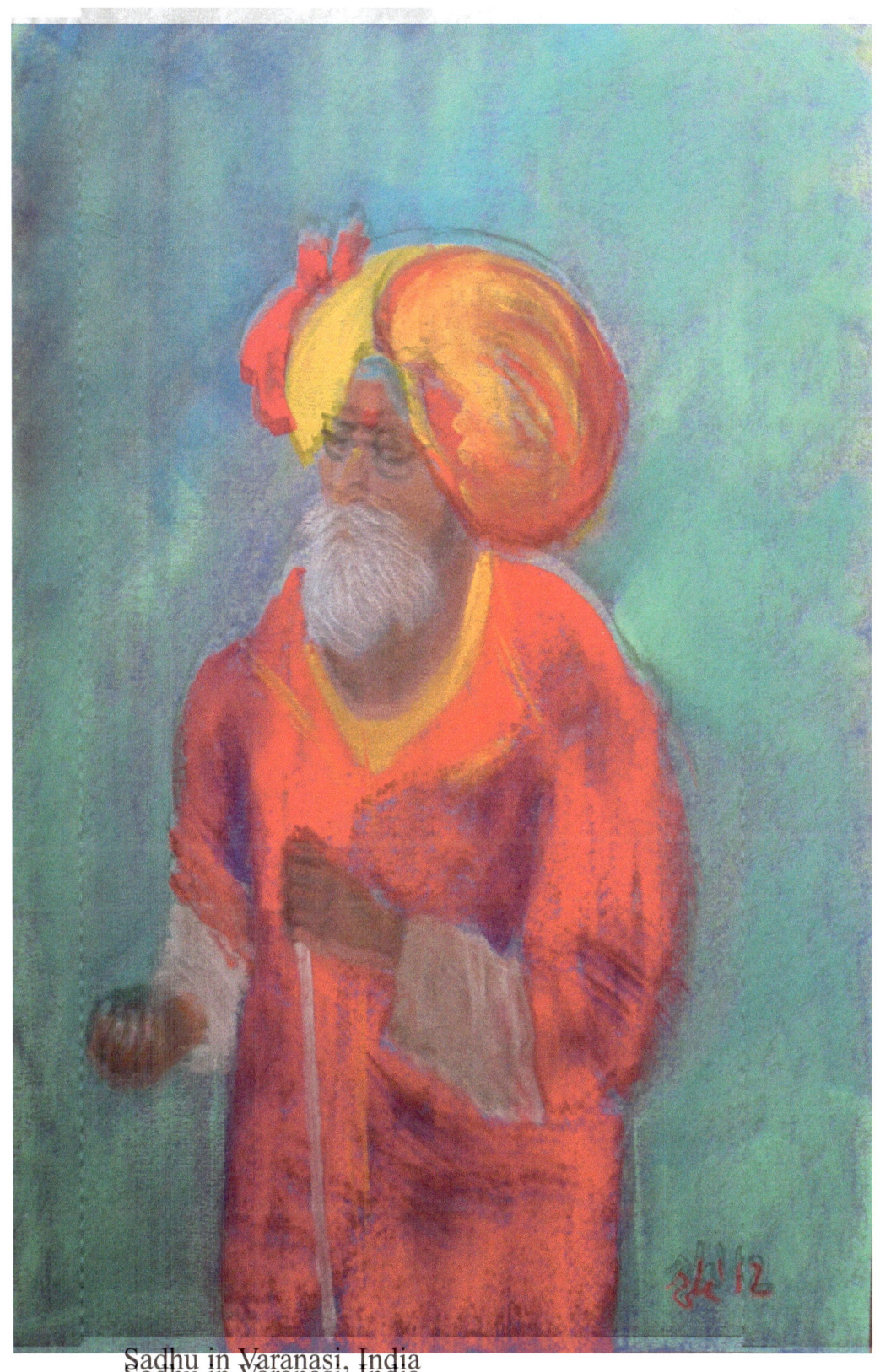

Sadhu in Varanasi, India
Sadhu in Varanasi, India

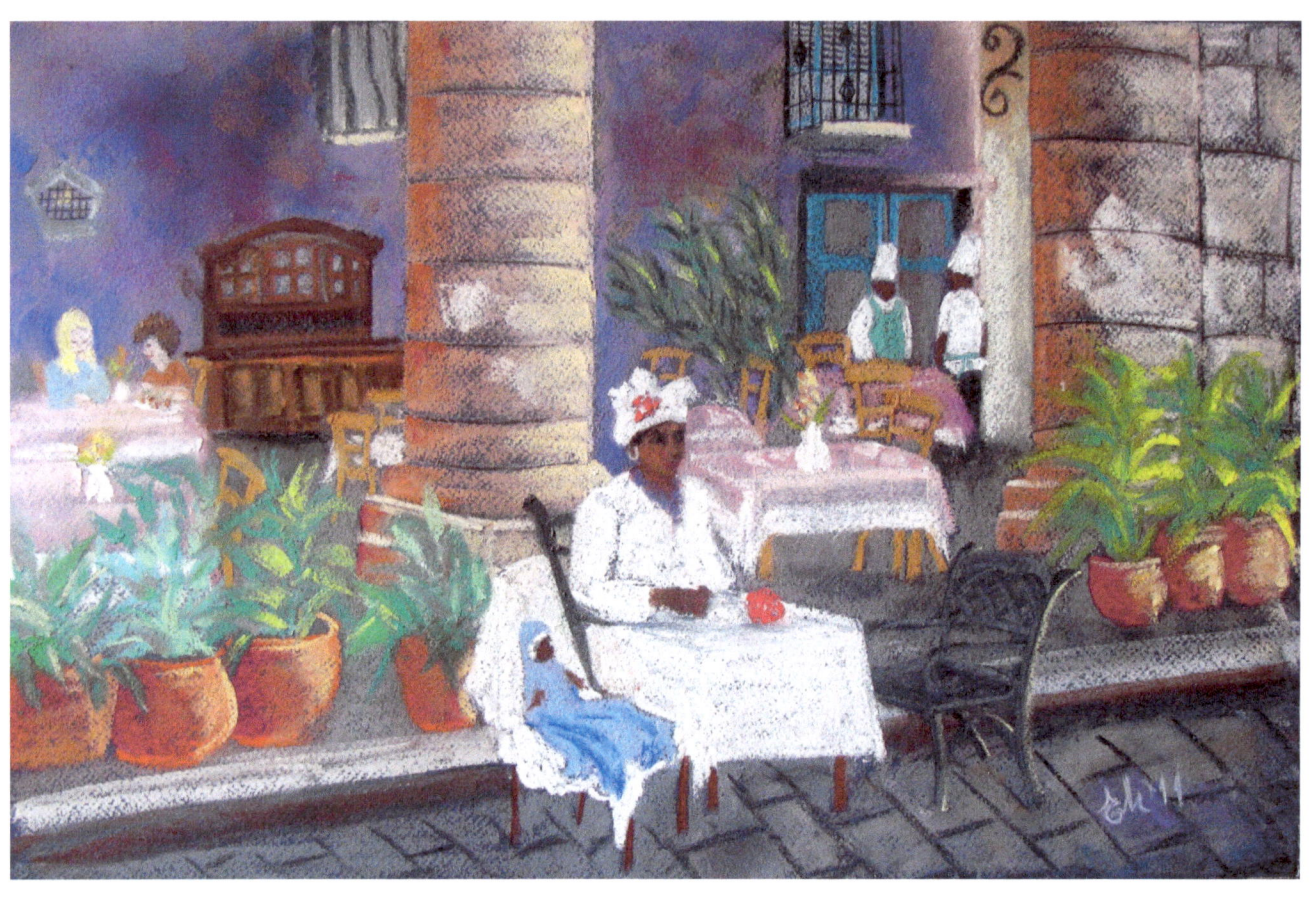

Santera in the cathedral square, Havana, Cuba

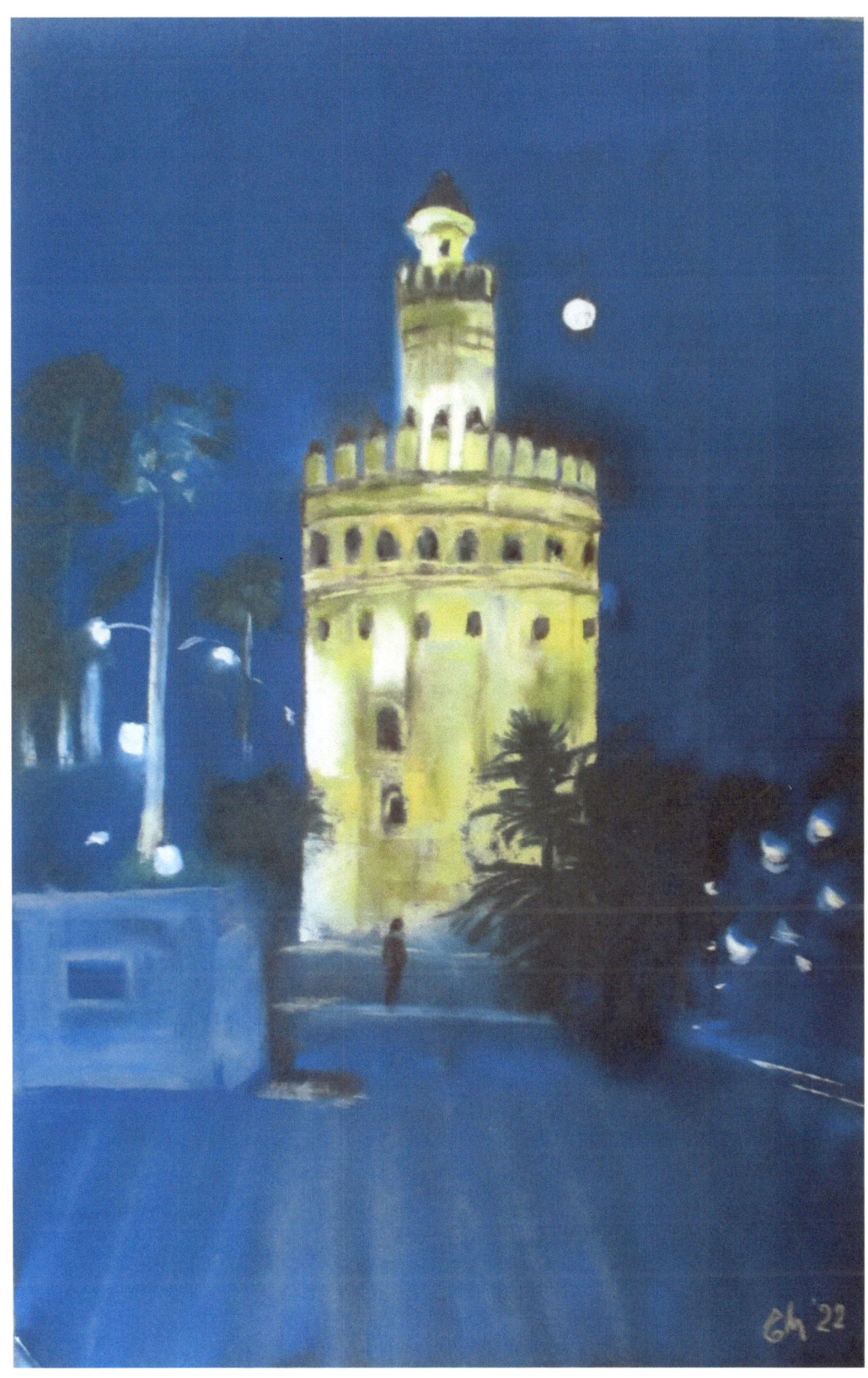

Seville by night, Spain

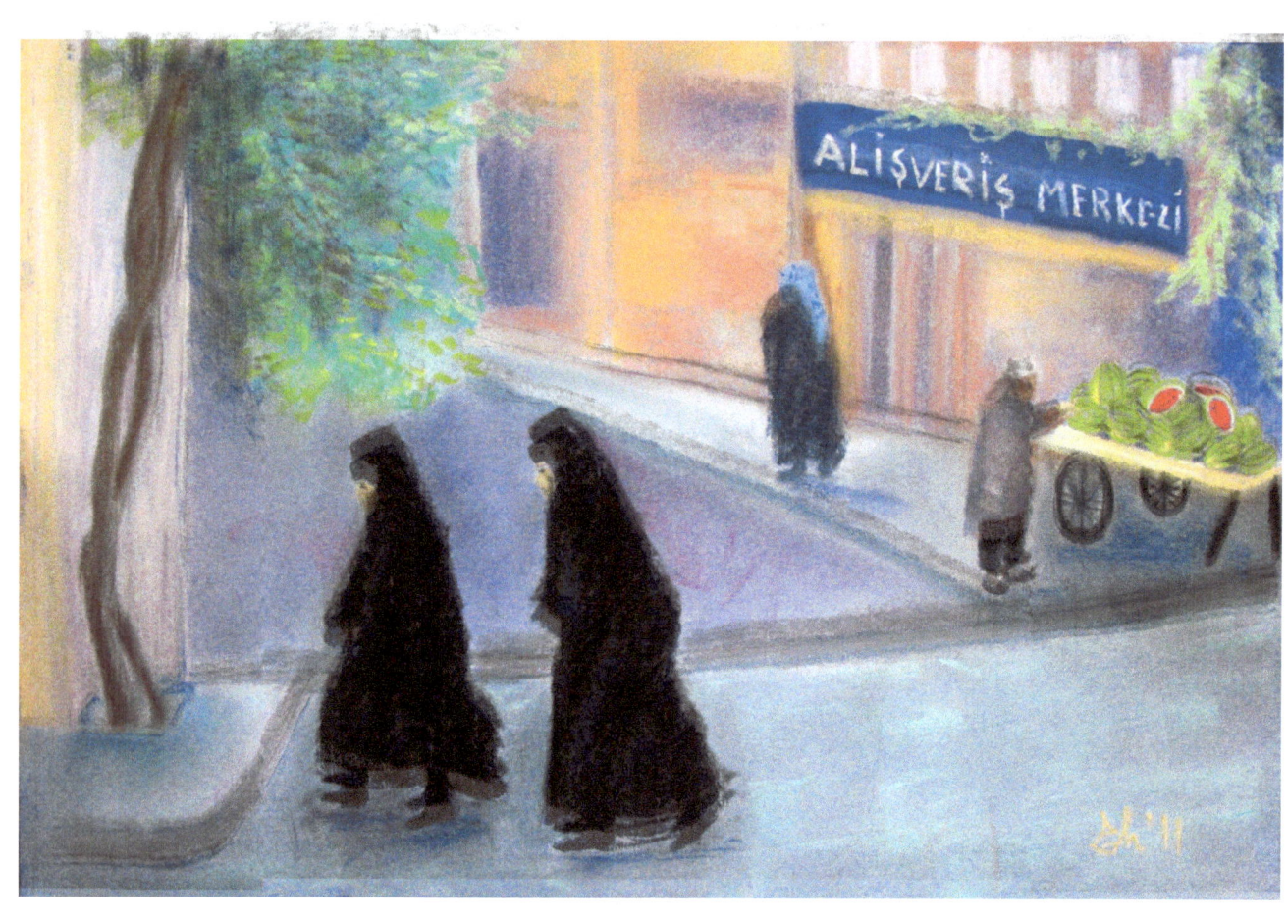

Street scene in Fanar, Istanbul, Turkiye
Street scene in Fanar, Istanbul, Turkiye

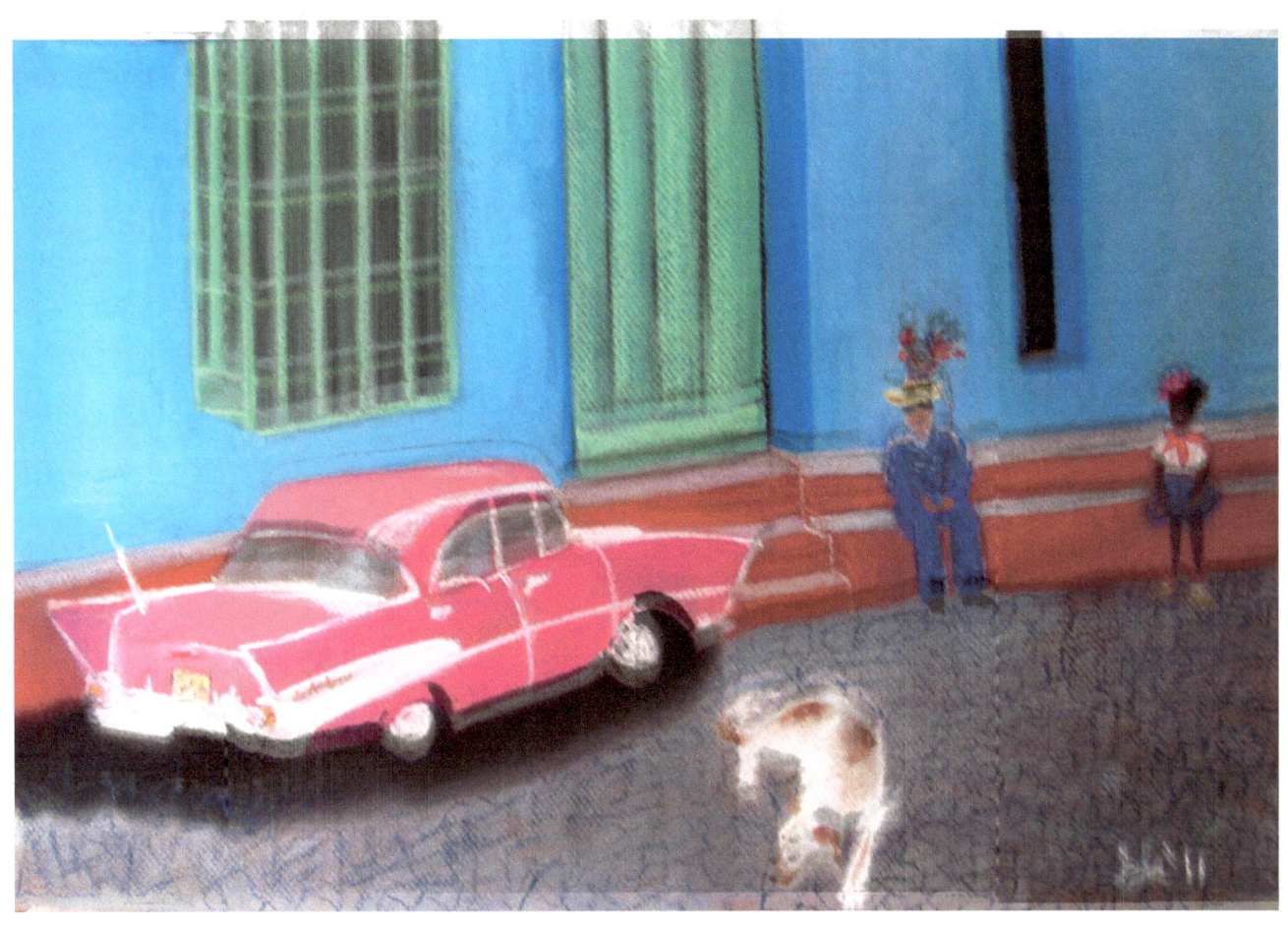

Street scene in Santiago de Cuba, Cuba

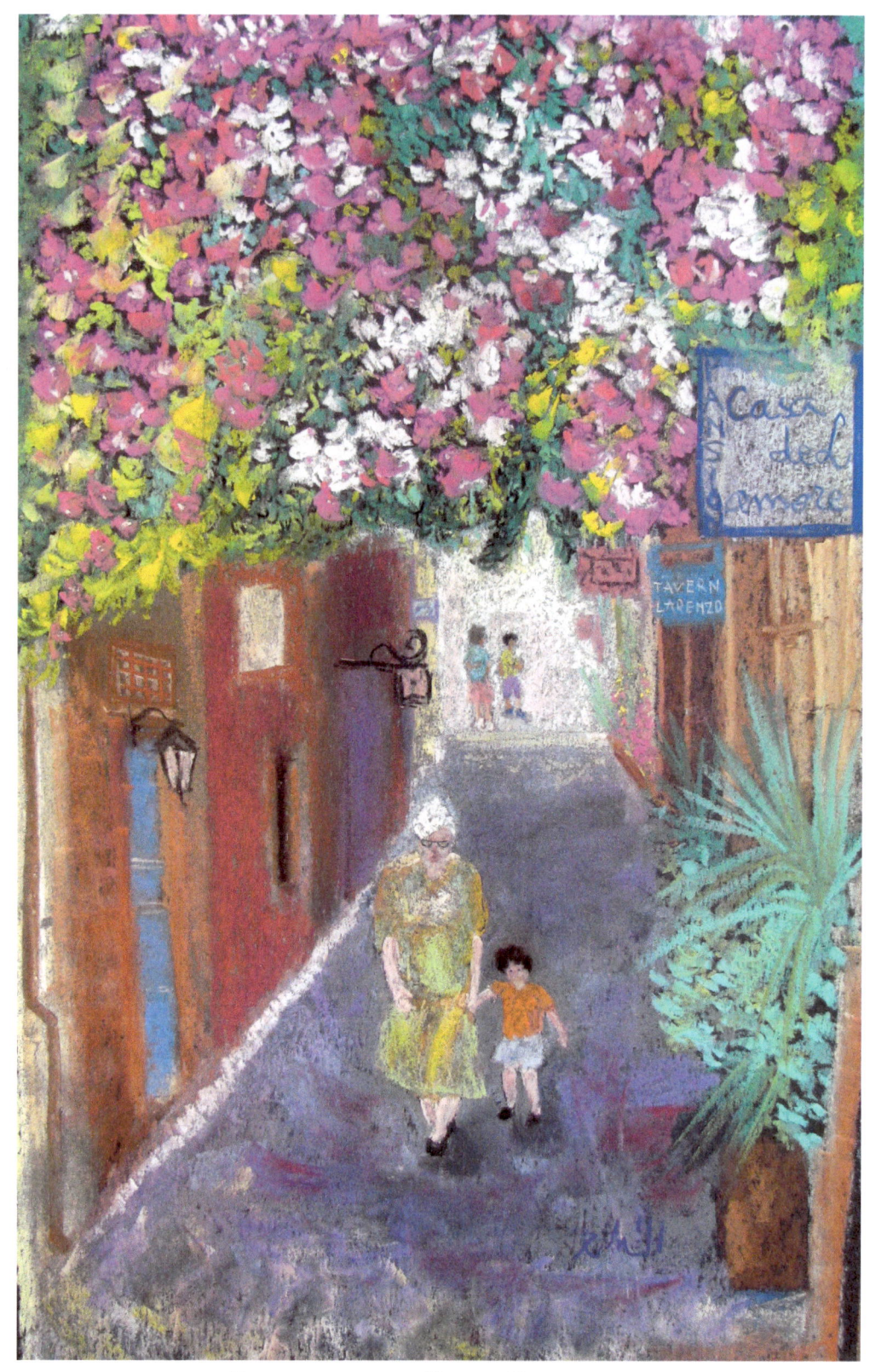

Street scene on Crete, Greece

Traditional syrup seller in Istanbul, Turkiye

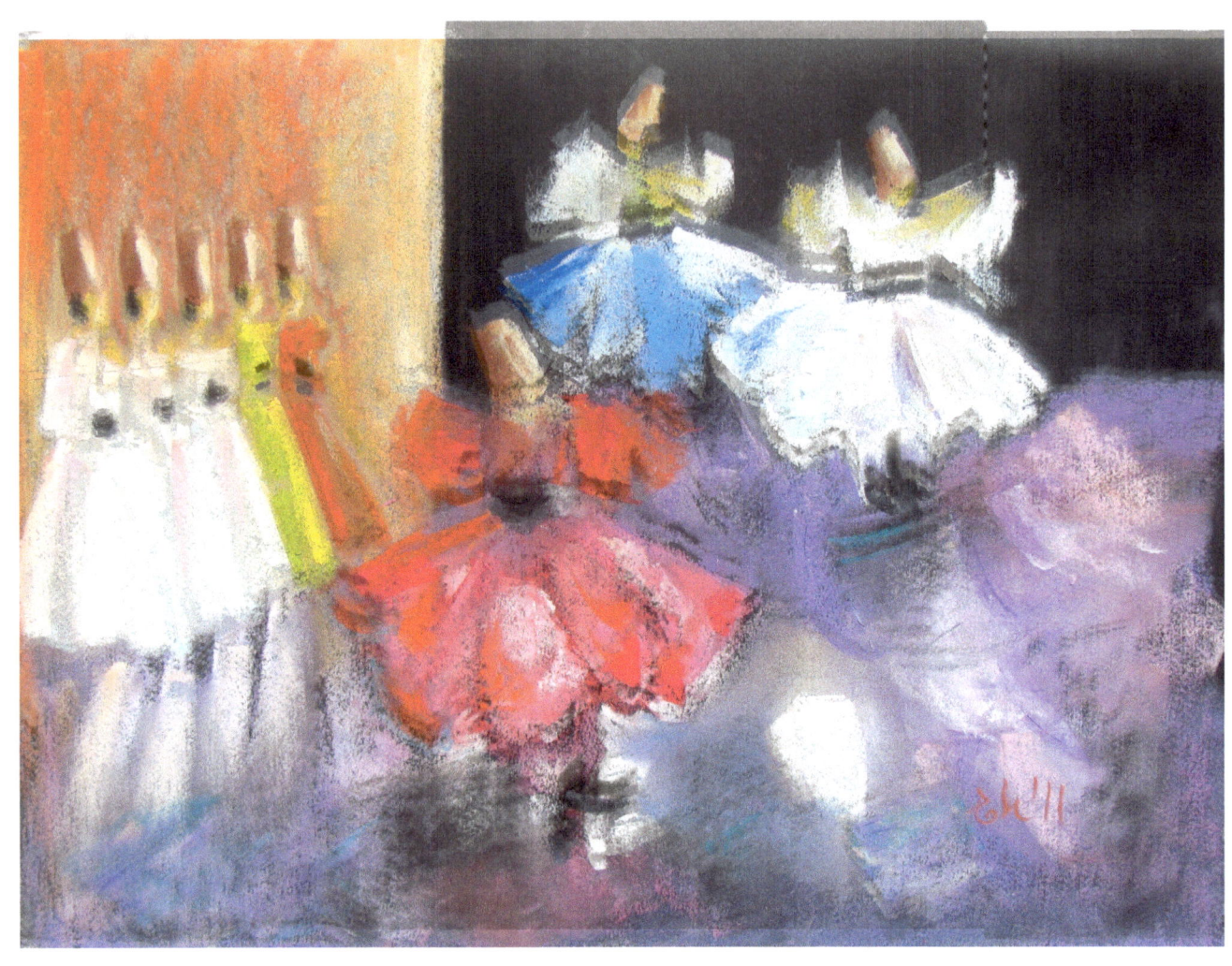

Whirling dervishes, Istanbul, Turkiye

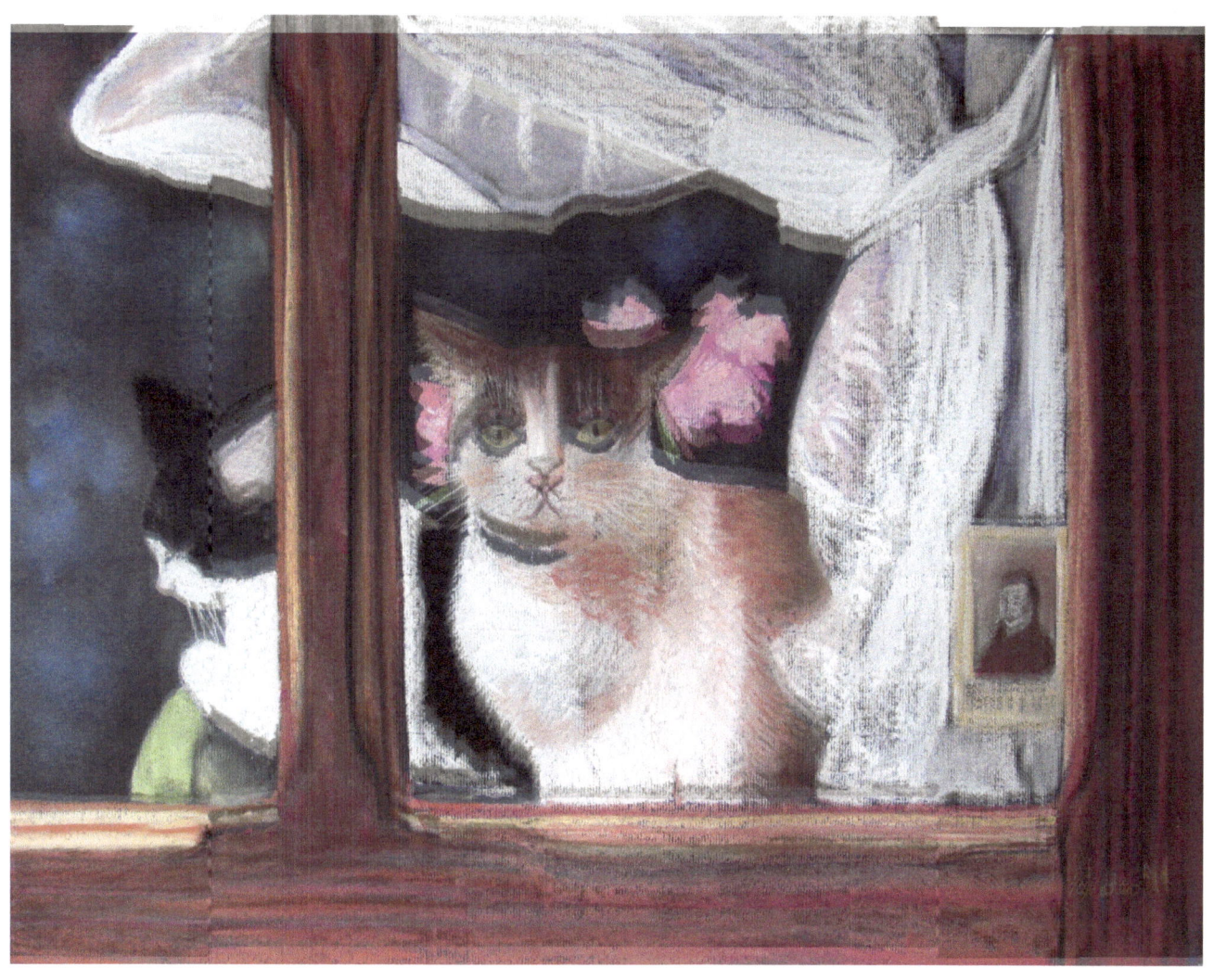

Window seats, Valencia, Spain
Window seats, Valencia, Spain

About this series and the artist

The series started in 2011 and continues through 2024. There are 45 pieces of different sizes and also supports like paper, sanded paper, mat board. Sizes vary between 9x12in to 22x28in. Only quality artist grade soft pastels have been used.

The source of inspiration are my travel photographs or composition from several photographs.

These pieces are not for sale. They document a place and a moment in time. They form a collection of scenes from life on earth in our century and should be displayed as a collection.

About the artist

I am a self-taught artist living in Southern California. Besides being a childhood passion, art making became my hobby in 2008, at 53 years of age, when I started learning from web resources and working in several mediums like graphite, charcoal, sketching pencils, mixed media, oil pastel, soft pastel, colored pencils, watercolor.

My artworks in the media mentioned above I documented in several art books, which are not instruction books but rather present my way with the respective medium and techniques.

Art offers me freedom of expression and through the visual quality of art I try to emphasize its universal appeal to peace and harmony.